To
Have Faith
Think Positive
Dick Vitale
HOF 08

NEVER GIVE UP

Copyright © 2023 SuccessBooks®

All rights reserved. No part of this book may be used or reproduced in any manner whatsoever without prior written consent of the author, except as provided by the United States of America copyright law.

Published by SuccessBooks®, Orlando, FL.

SuccessBooks® is a registered trademark.

Printed in the United States of America.

ISBN: 979-8-9862097-7-7
LCCN: 2023910209

This publication is designed to provide accurate and authoritative information with regard to the subject matter covered. It is sold with the understanding that the publisher is not engaged in rendering legal, accounting, or other professional advice. If legal advice or other expert assistance is required, the services of a competent professional should be sought. The opinions expressed by the authors in this book are not endorsed by SuccessBooks® and are the sole responsibility of the author rendering the opinion.

Most SuccessBooks® titles are available at special quantity discounts for bulk purchases for sales promotions, premiums, fundraising, and educational use. Special versions or book excerpts can also be created to fit specific needs.

For more information, please write:
SuccessBooks®
3415 W. Lake Mary Blvd. #950370
Lake Mary, FL 32746
or call 1.877.261.4930

NEVER GIVE UP

SuccessBooks®
Lake Mary, Florida

CONTENTS

CHAPTER 1
NEVER GIVE UP
By Dick Vitale 11

CHAPTER 2
OBSCURITY HAS ITS PLACE
By Peter 'Coach Pete' D'Arruda 27

CHAPTER 3
THE POWER TO OVERCOME
By Pat Ziemer 33

CHAPTER 4
WHAT BEN SAID
By Rick Barnett 41

CHAPTER 5
I NEVER EXPECTED TO BE DR. TERI
By Dr. Teri Rouse 49

CHAPTER 6
A LOVE STORY
By Patti Magan 59

CHAPTER 7
RISING FROM THE COLD
By Dr. Sam Nguyen 65

CHAPTER 8
THE *ADD* ADVANTAGE
By Dr. Fred Rouse 75

CHAPTER 9
UNBREAKABLE HOPE
By Gary Patti 83

CHAPTER 10
WOUNDED HEALER
By Jennifer Perri 93

CHAPTER 11
KEEP MOVING FORWARD: #KMF
By Guy Colangelo 99

CHAPTER 12
REAL ESTATE IN AN UNREAL YEAR
By Amber Noble 107

CHAPTER 13
THE GAME OF POSSIBILITY: SA-ME-ZA
By Bably Bhasin 115

CHAPTER 14
ECONOMICS OF LIFE
By Mark Wade 125

CHAPTER 15
IT'S NOT THE MOUNTAINS WE CONQUER
By Julie Meates 135

CHAPTER 16
YOU CAN ~~NEVER~~ GIVE UP
By Larry Kozin 145

CHAPTER 17
THE FREEDOM TO NEVER GIVE UP
By Kevin Hodes 153

CHAPTER 18
A TALE OF NO RETURNS
By Juan (Carlos) Samaniego 161

CHAPTER 19
WHEN I SAID I DO
THE BRENT AND SUSAN HAGGERTY STORY
By Brent Haggerty 171

CHAPTER 20
ONE POINT AT A TIME
By Nick Nanton 177

CHAPTER 21
THE SALE WAS A BONUS
By Richard Tyler 185

CHAPTER 22
WHEN A FALL BECOMES A LEAP
By Emigdio Arias 193

CHAPTER 23
THE OTHER SIDE OF THE MOUNTAIN
By Zack Viscomi 201

CHAPTER 24
MAGNIFY
By Stacey Johnson 207

CHAPTER 1

NEVER GIVE UP

BY DICK VITALE

I lost an eye when I was a kid—poked it with a pencil, leaving me blind in that eye for as long as I can remember. For decades it bothered me. It wasn't enough to lose the vision. The eye drifted on me. I could never look at a person eye-to-eye. I'd be looking with my good eye, and the person I'm talking to turns his head to see where the other eye is going.

As a kid it was tough to stand out like that, and I was embarrassed again and again. When I pitched in Little League games, parents would scream, "Does that kid know where he is throwing the ball? Look at his eye!"

Oh, my God, it was knives in me—the parents screaming at me like that. I would go home after games and sit in my room, shedding tear after tear. My mom and dad would come in and say, "Richie!" (It was never Dick. It was always Richie.) They'd say, "Richie, don't let them get the best of you!"

The love from my mom and dad really benefited me. One day I just said, "This is who I am, and I am going to do the best I can." And I have tried to have a sense of pride in what I do and to do everything to the best of my ability.

I recently started my 45th year at ESPN. I can't say my 45th year of work because it's not work when you love what you do. Work is what my dad did—at a factory, along with my mom, to support my brother and sister and me. And I'll tell you this: They really worked.

My dad pressed coats. The more coats he pressed in that big factory, the more dollars he made. So he was paid by piecework. And it was a sweat shop, man, a sweat shop. My mother would sew the coats, and then the coats would be brought over to my dad. He'd start early every morning, which taught me about punctuality. I would say to him, "Why go to work so soon?" He'd leave at 7 or 6:45 a.m. to start at 8 a.m. But the bottom line is, he was always early, and it rubbed off on me.

My mom eventually had a stroke. She could barely drag one leg, and yet she found a way to move. My dad would bring the coats home, and she would sew them down in the basement, going up and down our stairs on her injured leg.

I learned about work ethic from my parents, and they also gave me the desire to always be better today than yesterday. They instilled in me so much spirit. And they were my role models. They just had fifth-grade educations, but I always say they had doctorates in love.

SCHOOL DAZE

As a youngster, I was into sports more than anything. I would get the necessary grades in school to pass, but what I cared about was sports, sports, sports. I read column after column in the world of sports, especially in the New York metropolitan area.

I'll never forget what happened one day in my business class at East Rutherford High School. The teacher was Miss Lucy Zanca. She was giving a lecture, and I was in the back of the class reading a column by the famous sports writer Dick Young of the New York Daily News. Mr. Young wrote a dot-dot-dot column—a string of facts, comments, statistics, plays, and events separated by the dot-dot-dot…one item after another. He covered everything in sports, and I devoured it.

Well, I'm in the back of Miss Zanca's class reading his column, and I look up to see her running towards me. I tried to throw my paper down to protect it, but she was fast. She grabbed it, ripped it up, and started screaming at me: "Richie! You can be so bright! And yet the only thing you worry about is sports, sports, sports! Where is sports gonna take you?"

Oh man, I wish Ms. Zanca could see where sports have taken me!

I laugh now because I don't advise others to do in school what I did—certainly not my kids. My daughters, Terri and Sherri, were great students, following in their mom's footsteps. My wife, Lorraine, actually skipped her junior year in high school. That's how bright she is.

I managed to get into Seton Hall University in New Jersey, which I was grateful for, because coming out of the high school my grades were not the best. I got a business degree in accounting, and my first job out of college was in bookkeeping for a plumbing company in Paterson, New Jersey. I'd look around at other employees who might have been there 10, 20, even 25 years. They were all watching the clock, punching in every morning at eight and out every day at five. I'd say to myself, "Wow, I cannot see myself doing this all my life."

Then one day I got a great break. I was coaching a baseball team of athletes between ages 16 and 19, who I had recruited. I was on the field with them when an administrator for the schools in Garfield, New Jersey came over to me. He said, "I love the way you handle kids. Have you ever thought about teaching?"

My degree was in business. But this man said he could get me a job as an elementary school teacher with a provisional certificate. I could take credit hours at night to get certified in education. I was maybe 25 years old, and I said, "Are you kidding me? I'm on my way!"

Financially, it was a big difference. I made only $4,500 a year, but I was never happier. Besides teaching in elementary school, I coached three junior high teams in football, basketball, and baseball.

All I knew about football was that if the scoreboard said '6 to 0,' then we had to get to 7. And we always did. For two years we lost not one football game. We were 18 and 0. But I decided to specialize in basketball.

And one day the phone call came—another big break. The administrator of East Rutherford, my old high school, called me. On the call he said, "You're doing a heckuva job down here in Garfield. We'd like you to come back to East Rutherford, to your old high school. We're gonna make you head basketball coach, and you'll also teach middle school.'

I was on cloud nine. I said, "Head coach! Are you kidding me?"

"Before you get too excited," he said, "I want you to know that nobody wants the job. *Nobody.*"

I WANTED THE JOB

But he was wrong. I wanted the job. The old high school gym wasn't actually a gym, more like four stone walls with padding, and so small it had no out-of-bounds. We could practice in it, but couldn't play games, so every game was on the road, and none of that bothered me. I was just happy for the opportunity.

East Rutherford, at the time, was a football powerhouse, and its coach, Ken Sinofsky, was my idol. As a student I'd watch him walk the halls and say to myself, "Man, I would love one day to have kids look at me the way we all look at Coach Sinofsky." He was tough, and he was firm, but he was always fair. People had such respect and admiration for him.

I was lucky enough to play for him in high school, and then when I started coaching in my twenties, I picked up so much from Coach Sinofsky. I believe that played a big role in advancing me in the coaching profession.

My team at East Rutherford was a bunch of tough, blue-collar youngsters who played their hearts out. On our first day I told them, "We're not worried about building five years down the road. We're going to do it now." We started with running and nothing else. No basketball—just line drills and double sessions and conditioning, and they worked hard. I wanted to prepare them for anything that anyone could throw at them. By the time they got into a real game, they wouldn't have to think. Just by reflex they'd know what to do.

You could safely say my coaching style was like my announcing style. It had energy. Some of my players remember the refs forever telling me to step back, to move behind the line. I'd get so excited they'd toss me out of the game. And I won't lie: Some of the games gave me ulcers. But we started winning, and everybody in this football town got on board.

I had a winning attitude, the kids got a winning attitude, and it didn't stop with basketball. I wanted them to win as people. Every day for twenty minutes to half an hour I'd talk to them about life. Some of these kids had no fathers, so I'd talk to them personally, too, about things they needed to know and do to grow up.

I was also teaching sixth grade at Franklin School in East Rutherford, and it was the greatest time of my life. I wanted to show the students lots of love because that is what got me through my tough times.

My parents, as I said, had doctorates in love. My brother, sister, and I learned so much from them just sitting around the dinner table. The one thing I will never forget from my parents was something they'd say to me all the time. They'd say: "Richie, treat people how you want to be treated."

If we all did that, we would have more love in our nation There is just not enough love in our world today.

In East Rutherford, the team with no home games won basketball championships two years in a row. Back-to-back, baby! When the state tournament came, it so happened that we had the number-one player in all of New Jersey. Les Cason was 6'10", a terrific talent getting recruited all over the country. He led us to a state title and had one of the greatest championship games any player could have, in a one-point win.

Unfortunately, in his personal life, Les made some bad decisions and got in with the wrong crowd. He died at a young age due to the drug scene, and it still crushes me. One of the big pains in my heart and my life is that Les never became the player I believed he could be.

FIVE STAR CAMP IN THE POCONOS

What ultimately took me out of East Rutherford, New Jersey was a man known as Howard Garfinkel, head of the Five Star Basketball Camp in the Poconos. Among coaches Howard was a superstar, and everyone knew him. Name a major player of the time, anyone from Michael Jordan to Patrick Ewing, and he went to The Five Star Basketball Camp, where 'Garf' connected college coaches from around the country to America's top young basketball talent.

What a scene it was. During the week of camp, Garf would bring in three speakers, always a big deal. And one day I was one of those speakers, addressing hundreds of players in the camp's airplane-hanger gym. When Five Star Garf heard me, he took me aside and said, "You belong in college."

I was honest with him. I told him I'd sent out a lot of letters, and it just wasn't happening. I was a sixth-grade teacher and high school coach making $12,000 a year and wanting to coach college. And now Howard Garfinkel, who's seen several of his camp workers go on to college basketball, was telling me I belonged in college.

He said to me, "I'm talking to Rutgers. They just got a new head coach, Dick Lloyd, and they'll be looking for their staff."

Howard called up Dick Lloyd, and asked him to interview me. Dick said he had already interviewed several people and would decide on one that week, but he agreed to interview me as a favor. I figured meeting him would be a good experience even if there was no shot of getting that job. And then I went to the interview, and I was on cloud nine. Dick even took me by his house to meet his family.

Later that day, I got home and the phone rang, and it was Dick Lloyd. He said he wasn't wasting any time, and he wanted to hire me.

I couldn't believe it. Tears rolled down my face. My wife, Lorraine, and I went out to dinner that night at Barcelona's in Garfield, New Jersey—the same spot my parents used to take our family to on Friday nights. Lorraine asked me what Rutgers was paying me, and I realized I had never asked. Turns out I was taking a $1,000 pay cut to $11,000 a year, but I didn't care. I was in college ball now, baby!

RUTGERS AND A FINAL FOUR APPEARANCE

Rutgers had never made the NCAA tournament, and it had no superstars. That was its problem. At my first meeting with the other coaches, I remember looking at the players we planned to recruit and saying to my bosses, "Who are we going to beat? I want to beat the great teams. If you think you're mediocre, you'll be mediocre."

There was no reason we couldn't be special. We were in a great area—New York City, Philadelphia, New Jersey—surrounded by talent. I began recruiting, going after the best, and I got lucky.

People told me I was wasting my time pursuing a kid by the name of Phil Sellers, the superstar from Thomas Jefferson High School in Brooklyn. "You got no shot," they'd say. "Every big-name school in the country wants this guy."

Well, I got a commitment from Phil, who went on to become the leading scorer in the history of Rutgers. And from there it snowballed. We got Mike Dabney, the best player in New Jersey, who everyone thought was headed to the University of Dayton. He'd never so much as watched a Rutgers basketball game. But I had a vision, and I never gave up. I committed to seeing his games and to trying to show him the big picture.

In 1976, Mike Dabney and Phil Sellers led Rutgers to the Final Four, competing against Indiana, UCLA, and Michigan and what an experience that was for Rutgers.

When Dick Lloyd left Rutgers, he recommended me for the head coach job, and I would have loved the opportunity. I practically begged for it, saying I would take it even at my same assistant salary. But the higher-ups wanted someone with more experience, so they hired Tom Young, who was successful at American University. And it turned out for the best. A chance encounter was about to lead me to my next gig and first position as head coach.

UNIVERSITY OF DETROIT TO THE BIG LEAGUES

After losing out on the Rutgers position, I was hanging out one day with my dear friend Willis Reed, who played center for the New York Knicks. We were in the team locker room when Knicks superstar Dave DeBusschere walked by.

Willis introduced us, and in the small talk Dave asked what I was up to these days. I told him I was looking for a head coaching job, and he said his alma mater, The University of Detroit, was looking for a new coach. Willis told him to put in a call for me, and I laughed it off.

Well, would you believe it? About 10 days later I get a phone call from someone saying they want to interview me for the job in Detroit. Then they offered me the job, and accepting it was the best decision I could have made. I moved my family from New Jersey to Detroit to coach the Detroit Titans. The team was full of talent and great people—outstanding people who I stay in touch with to this day.

On the competitive front, the unbelievable happened. In my final year as head coach we won 21 games in a row. We made it to the Sweet 16 before losing to Michigan, then the number one team in the country.

But that game also changed my life again.

At that Sweet 16 game, UCLA Coach John Wooden and broadcaster Curt Gowdy came over to speak with me. They were there analyzing and doing play-by-play for the NBC broadcast of our game. They liked my energy and enthusiasm, and they mentioned me later to a guy by the name of Scotty Connal—telling him he should think about getting me into TV. More on that later.

From coaching at the University of Detroit, my career continued to skyrocket. In 1978, I was 39 years old and hired by the Detroit Pistons. From high school to the NBA in such a short time was a whirlwind, but the bottom line is that it didn't work out. I was fired from the head coach position with the Detroit Pistons on November 8, 1979. In that league, you can't win every game, and man, I hated losing. I couldn't handle losing, and now I was out of a job.

THANK GOD IT DIDN'T WORK OUT

When the Pistons fired me, I went into a depression. I hung around home watching Luke and Laura on *General Hospital* until Lorraine kicked me in the butt. She said, "You can whine and feel sorry for yourself, or you get can get back your pride and your passion and go out and make something happen in your life."

And then a phone call came. The voice on the line said, "Dick, you're not going to remember me. My name is Scotty Connal. I was the guy in charge of the production for NBC when Curt Gowdy and John Wooden covered your game in that tough loss to Michigan."

He kept talking. "After the game, as we left the arena, Coach Wooden and Curt Gowdy said to me, 'Scotty, we love that guy's energy, his enthusiasm. You should think about him in TV.' So I wrote your name down," Scotty said. "I've just been named head of a new network called ESPN, and I'd like you to do our first game."

I'll be honest with you. My first reaction was, "What's ESPN? Sounds like a disease." But all I said was no thank you, because I wanted to get back to coaching in college, where I felt I belonged.

Lucky for me, ten days before the game, Scotty called again, and my wife practically chased me out of the house. She said, "You are violating everything you preach about pride, work ethic, and desire—sitting here moping because things didn't go your way. Go do the game and have fun. Just talk basketball."

So I told him I'd do it. And I announced that first game for ESPN on December 5, 1979: DePaul vs. Wisconsin. I knew absolutely nothing about TV, but I fell in love with it. And I was lucky to be paired with Hall of Fame announcer Jim Simpson, who helped me learn the art of getting in and out during a telecast.

Announcing played into so many things I loved. I was a former coach, fresh out of the gym. I knew the X's and O's. I knew about relationships and coaching and how to watch a game—how to think through a game. The fact that I got fired as a coach made me a human being, relatable. Coaches have a language with one another, a level of respect.

And the networks listened in to this baldheaded, one-eyed guy, and decided they'd like me to keep talking.

JUST YOUR AVERAGE BALD, ONE-EYED, BASKETBALL WACKO WHO BEAT THE ZIGGY AND BECAME A PTP'ER

God has a way of blocking your path to send you in a new direction.

At first, I was sure announcing was a temporary gig until I could get back to coaching. But here I am, going on my 45th year with ESPN, and I have loved every day. As a career it has exceeded any dream I ever had. I can't run, jump, or shoot, and as I tell people, "I've got a body by linguini, but I am in 14 Hall of Fames because all my life I've tried to put passion and pride in everything I do."

Lorraine always knew where I belonged. When I worked a game, she'd say, "You're talking to your people…folks there to see a game…the everyday person just having fun."

When a game's over, I never watch the winning coach walk out. I watch the losing coach, and I say to myself, "Man, I don't want to be in his shoes today." I know how tough it is in the media world with the online stuff, the radio talk shows…the pressure is unbelievable.

I know the pain of that scrutiny. When my colleagues and I went in for studio work in the early days, we'd walk out and ask the receptionist if anyone called. You know you're hitting a home run if people are phoning in.

On one of those studio days we walked out and the receptionist said, "No calls today except for one guy. I'm so mad about him."

I said, "What are you mad about?"

She says, "He wants to get ahold of the president of our company because he wants you off the air. He can't stand looking at you with your eye." Oh, my God, that knife again—right through me. I was back in Little League with the parents screaming to pull me out of the game.

Sometime after that, my wife took my daughters to their annual eye test. The doctor sees Lorraine's name and says, "By any chance do you know Dick Vitale?" "I know him well," she says. "He's my husband."

"Really?" the doc says. "I'm a big basketball fan. I can straighten that eye out. No problem. I know I can."

So I went to the doc, and he made me the same promise. "Just one thing," he says, "and I don't want you to get nervous, but to straighten out your bad left eye, I also have to operate on your good eye.

"You have to sign papers," he said, "God forbid something should happen."

"Are you kidding me?" I may have shouted. "End of conversation! I can't take a chance on the vision in my good eye!" I went home, and I tossed and turned and tossed and turned. Finally I said to Lorraine, "I'm going to go for it."

I went into that surgery as scared as I've ever been in my life... *In my life*. When I came out of the it, the doc said, "Everything's fine. You can relax." It was the best thing I could have done, and it changed my whole life.

PASSION + PRIDE + PERSEVERANCE

As many of you know, I recently battled multiple cancers; melanoma and lymphoma. In the midst of it, I had two vocal cord surgeries, and I lost my voice for many weeks. Through it all I kept hearing the words of Jimmy Valvano: "Don't give up... don't ever give up."

Jimmy was an outstanding coach who became my ESPN colleague, and a dear friend who died of metastatic cancer. He announced the start of The V Foundation for Cancer Research in 1993 at the first-ever ESPY Awards, when he had two months to live. He also announced the foundation's motto that day: 'Don't give up...don't ever give up.'

I had the honor of walking Jimmy to the stage that night to give his speech. Who would have thought then that his foundation would raise more than $310 million in his memory to help people battling cancer.

Another highlight of my life was at the Sports Emmys in 2022, when I received the Jimmy V Award for Perseverance. On the stage that night, I shared the formula I believe in so much: "Passion + pride + perseverance = a win in the game of life. A game we all play."

During my months of chemotherapy, when my family would leave for the night, I'd be in the room by myself, and I would hear the words, "Don't give up. Don't ever give up." I'd also hear the words my mom said to me as a youngster. "Don't you ever, ever believe in 'can't,'" she'd say. "You can be what you want to be. You have energy, you have enthusiasm, and you have a passion for everything you do. Keep doing that, and good things are going to happen."

THE GAME OF LIFE

Looking back at my life, I've been blessed. I married the beautiful young Lorraine McGrath in 1971. We met at a singles club called the Blue Swan in Rochelle Park, New Jersey. She was there with her girlfriends after work. I'd come in with some coaching buddies, and they bet me she wouldn't dance with me. Sure enough, when I asked her, she said she'd just come to be with her friends.

She turned me down several times, but finally she said yes, and we've been dancing ever since.

It's been 52 years of marriage so far. We have two beautiful daughters, Terri and Sherri, and five incredible grandchildren. Nothing is more important to me than family, and I am blessed with a wonderful one. When I battled cancer, my family got me through the tough times.

And yet those times were nothing, *nothing*, compared to what other people face. And now more than ever—I want to help in their fight. Every week, 350 moms and dads will go home and hear four words that no parent ever wants to hear, "Your child has cancer." And I promise you, until my last breath, I will beg and I will plead to forever put an end to those words.

The annual gala I host to help fund research for kids battling cancer has raised more than $60 million. That support is the most important thing I will ever do. For Jimmy, and more than ever for myself, I want to raise the support that will change parents' lives by giving them back the lives of their kids.

My life hit reset when I was told by my doctors on April 21, 2022 that I was cancer free. It was unbelievable. When you get to remission, the tradition is to ring a bell at the hospital. Did I ring the bell? I rang it so hard, I *broke the bell, baby.* It was like my national championship.

I've had one unbelievable journey, and I'm grateful. I try to treat every day like the most important day of my life and be better each day than I was yesterday. That's a message I share through my motivational speaking and the message I want to share with anyone reading this now:

Chase your dreams, and chase your goals. Be the best you can be, each and every day. Do that, and you're a winner in the biggest game of all, the game we all play, the game of life.

About Dickie V

Dick Vitale's passion, knowledge, and over-the-top enthusiasm for the game of basketball is known worldwide. College basketball's top analyst and ambassador, Vitale joined ESPN during the 1979-80 season shortly after the network's launch.

Since then, he has called over 1,000 games. In 2008 he received the sport's ultimate honor when he was selected as an inductee into the Naismith Memorial Basketball Hall of Fame.

"I'm living the American dream," Vitale once said. "I learned from my mom and dad, who didn't have a formal education but both had a 'doctorate of love'. They told me that if you give 110 percent all of the time, a lot of beautiful things will happen. I may not always be right, but no one can ever accused me of not having a genuine love and passion for whatever I do."

Vitale is also a philanthropist. He's on the Board of Directors of The V Foundation, raising over $310 million for cancer research in memory of the late Jim Valvano. Dick hosts the annual Dick Vitale Gala with hundreds of supporters and celebrities to raise money for groundbreaking advancements in childhood cancer research. Attendees include Mike Krzyzewski, Buster Posey, Nick Saban, Dabo Swinney, Robin Roberts, Tony Dungy and many more. Thus far, the Dick Vitale Gala has raised over $68.1 million for pediatric cancer research.

Dick Vitale received the highest honor in sports broadcasting, winning the prestigious Lifetime Achievement Award at the 2019 Sports Emmys. He is only the second analyst to be recognized with this award after John Madden. He also received the 2022 ESPY'S Jimmy V Award for Perseverance.

CHAPTER 2

OBSCURITY HAS ITS PLACE

BY PETER 'COACH PETE' D'ARRUDA

First about my name. Early on, I was teaching teachers how to plan for retirement. At one of the schools, a principal got on the loudspeaker to broadcast my arrival, came to "D'Arruda," and detoured around it.

"Coach Pete will be here at 3 o'clock," he said, and the moniker stuck because that's me, a coach to the bone. Or you could say this apple fell and rolled to the base of the tree. My mom taught grade school. My dad taught college-level physics and astronomy. No one had to tell me that a teacher could know everything there is to know about Civil War artillery, sentence structure, or mass and energy, and fail an introductory quiz on how to manage monthly income into a reasonable retirement free of worries.

I'm repeatedly amazed that 99.9 percent of Americans walk out of high school with no money literacy, as if a person prepares for a profession but stumbles into how a paycheck takes us to old age, or not, and can even make dreams come true.

Early in my career I sponsored free steak dinners to pan for clients.

I sold insurance, I was a mortgage broker, and I got certified in money management. I taught small groups of intelligent people how to also be smart with their finances. Now I teach people who are savvy in finance how to get their points across without overtalking or over-educating. My 'never give up' story is about dreams and drive—in my case, how my drive to educate came true, or how financial coaching led to media coaching.

One piece of business first: Before writing this chapter, I contractually agreed to disclose the secret to my success, and here it is: The X factor is fun. If you entertain, I tell my broadcasters, you get paid like Mark Wahlberg. To teach about money and make a good living, you must also inform, engage, update, discuss, identify, encourage, debate, explain—*and amuse*. Because finance is not a lecture—it's life. It's current events, preparation, science, history, decision making, psychology, you name it. A good teacher links money to life and does it in word pictures, to salt the dish without over-salting. By that I mean a financial speaker should sprinkle only enough information for listeners to want more, because at the end of the day, individual people require individual financial counsel. On the air it's tempting to show off all you know, I tell my speakers, but everything you can say is not all a person needs.

My 31-year road from financial coaching to media coaching has taken me from a cinderblock station on a rural highway to a hundred financial advisors airing around the country. My never-give-up message comes from two years of those three decades in which I had almost no money and lived on credit cards. Then, on a good day, my influence covered maybe a 30-mile radius. But obscurity has its place. Two years in a one-man station in rural North Carolina became my on-the-job doctoral course in advanced financial communications.

As a kid out of college, finance came to me slantways, in conversations and observation. I observed, for example, that my girlfriend's father could golf on a weekday because he sold insurance. I saw home ownership mattered. I overheard the money struggles of people I loved. By the time I was 36 years old, I knew finance from the bottom up and the inside out, having immersed myself in every book I could find and trailing the smartest guys in the room like Steve Forbes and Warren Buffett.

What I learned I felt compelled to teach, but how to throw a net? How to reach people? Steak dinners and seminars go only so far, and I wasn't getting far otherwise. When I visited the big radio station in Raleigh with my idea for a financial show, an assistant met me in the lobby to say every single person on staff was busy and I could leave a resume.

"I'm not looking for work," I said looking around frustrated. "I came about doing a radio show." The assistant was sorry but no openings.

A few months later, on a drive back from a client meeting, on a stretch of road long on quiet and short on scenery, I saw a small cinderblock building with a big radio tower and the letters WEEB.

Why not? I tapped the brake and pulled into a one-man station owned and run by one Steve Adams, and we hit it off. Next thing I have an hour-long program on Saturdays at 3 p.m. More to the point, I had an assigned desk in Audience Building 101 because, of course, I had no idea what I was doing. I called my show the Money Hour, and my style was technical. I was the expert, right? I proceeded to preach, to teach, to show off what I knew.

I can tell you the day that changed. Station Owner Steve and I were in the same studio with two microphones. I was talking away, breaking down investing, maybe, or the dark fundamentals of credit card debt. The subject was complex, that I'm sure of, and there's a robust chance I was adding to the complexity. Glancing at Steve, I saw that his eyelids were down. His chin was about to hit to his chest, and…*stop frame*. If the station owner can't stay awake, what about my listeners in their cars? I was there to improve lives, not put drivers at risk.

Funny what you'll do to get people to stay awake. I invented terms like 'financial cruise control' for lifetime income plans. In the old gas stations, as you drove in, a ding-dong sounded to alert the attendant. On my show I'd call annual lifetime income checks 'financial fill-ups' to replenish the year, and I'd sound that ding-dong. Fees and commissions I called financial termites, hidden fees that eat away at our gains. No more 'the-market-is-up-the-market-is-down' reports. I was a financial comedian hosting the unfinancial financial hour. Every point had to apply to my listeners, and my world shifted on its axis.

The people in my audience weren't dozing at the wheel. They lived in beautiful homes all around that little town, they had money, and they wanted to learn. Just as important, they started calling in. One day the 'cricket line' at the station rang. The next day it rang more, and then the ringing took over.

"We love your show," callers would say. "There's nothing like it, and we love the information." I changed my show's name to 'The Financial Safari' because people in the wild need a guide and 'safari' is more interesting. More people tuned in, and more people were learning. Heck, I was learning—making mistakes, making changes…we were all learning together.

Another staple of broadcast communication is 'word of mouth.' Steve talked to some guys at a religious station in Raleigh who put me on the air and started getting more listeners than the other city stations. Remember the big one with no time to talk to me? We have seven hours of weekend programming on that station now.

Once the show began airing in Raleigh, other advisors began asking me how to do a radio show. Eventually I said to myself, "I need to stop giving free information and build my own radio network and offer the whole package of how to get on a station." I assembled a turnkey program and became a radio coach. I hired technicians and hosted advisors across the nation for 40 minutes or an hour until I was booked Monday through Thursday. So I hired more radio hosts and handed them the questions for the advisors each week. I taught my advisors to answer with the five W's and an H – who, what, where, when, why, and how—over the course of the conversation. Interviewers ask, and advisors keep the answers entertaining. Listeners learn, and companies hired me to do platforms for their institutions.

My objective is to clear the confusion, to un-muddy the waters, to get people to retirement without worry. There's so much misinformation out there, so many scams. I spend more time cleaning up other advisors' messes than starting from scratch. You saw the messes with FTX and Bernie Madoff. How does anyone know the information they get is right?

That brings us back to the teachers at the start of this chapter. Too many people get close to retirement with no idea whether they can comfortably retire without running out of money. I think of my dad teaching astronomy in college. What is the opposite of astronomy? Horoscopes. Instead of superstition, my dad taught people to see and know and understand the stars and planets in the night sky.

That's what I do. I teach people to give up superstition and magic and quick fixes. Money works on natural laws, on knowledge and informed decisions. In radio, in podcasts, on TV shows, and online, we entertain people into that kind of wisdom. Our net is massive, the financial world is always changing, and every day is different.

We can do it because at a cinderblock station on Interstate Nowhere a guy named Steve Adams had time for a guy bursting at the seams to find an audience.

So **never give up**. And never lose gratitude.

(...and to think Steve and I went to rival colleges – we shouldn't even be friends!)

About 'Coach Pete'

Peter J. D'Arruda, MRFC®, RICP®, is a Registered Financial Consultant and Investment Advisor Representative, and is Manager and Founding Principal of Capital Financial Advisory Group, LLC in Apex, North Carolina. A fiduciary with decades of experience in the financial services industry, he is the former two-time President of the IARFC (International Association of Registered Financial Consultants).

Known as 'Coach Pete' to most of his clients and to the listeners of his radio show, his lifetime goal is to assist his clients in achieving the levels of success they desire. He founded Capital Financial to help his clients 'cross the street of life.' He and his team strive to help their clients take the worry out of living in retirement by taking a systematic approach to lifetime income planning.

Coach Pete's radio show, *Financial Safari*, can be heard weekly on more than 70 stations nationwide. He has been a guest on CNBC, FOX Business, Bloomberg, and CBS Radio. He has been interviewed for advice on columns in *The Wall Street Journal, USA Today, Smart Money, Money, The Street.com*, as well as others.

He has been named to the prestigious Forbes Leadership Council and has been a published writer with Forbes.

Coach Pete has written or co-written eight books to date, and two of his books have reached the bestseller's list on Amazon. He co-authored the best-selling book *Tax Breaks of the Rich and Famous* and the noteworthy *SUCCESSONOMICS* with Steve Forbes. Coach Pete has also written his own popular books such as *Fine Print Fiasco* and *7 Baby Steps to a Ridiculously Reliable Retirement Income*.

Pete is a graduate of The University of North Carolina.

CHAPTER 3

THE POWER TO OVERCOME

BY PAT ZIEMER

In second grade I was held back, which is a hard thing for a kid, for reasons that no one knew until I was an adult and my son had my same reading difficulties.

In school I was called slow and had to find my own way, but with the words "Let's test you too," from my son's doctor, a new day dawned. I had *dyslexia*. Where most people see the words on a page in logical order, my mind saw them in reverse. In my work to absorb the words, mentally reorder them, and process the meaning, by a second page I was ready to fall asleep.

But little could I know that the skills I was picking up to compensate for my 'problems' would launch me in life—starting with collaboration skills. I finished college, for instance, not just on brain power but because my (future) wife and her best friend agreed to tutor me through Chemistry, Math, and English to a 2.5 average. As I matured, I'll add, so did my reading comprehension. My family owned funeral homes, and by the end of mortuary school, my 4.9 GPA was all mine.

What made me different in school felt like a flashing neon

'Dummy' sign over my desk, and yet my story turns on my savvy detours around that sign. As the big guys in my class showcased sports, I picked up the drums and joined a touring band that released *Shortening Bread* by the Villains, which landed in the Top 100. We were never big time, not quite, but we opened for groups like the Beach Boys. And I couldn't have said it then, but it was my family's community prominence fueling my need for my own image. Music and drums became my first course in never giving up.

College is where my minuses moved into the plus column. I was head of student government. I started the first fraternity at the University of Southern Indiana—Tau Kappa Epsilon—and was its first president. Since second grade, every time I came to something I couldn't do, I'd double up on what I could do, making me a doer, and to be honest, at times an over-doer. While others may idle their engines—I lived in fourth gear.

From mortuary school I went into the funeral business with my brother, where our eleven-years age difference came out as conflicting agendas. Ten years in, I sold my interest to him and built a marketing business, consulting with an industry magazine called *Pizza Today*. When *Pizza Today* sold to a New York company, I was out of work. But by now, I knew I could sell.

I shifted to aviation, to Lear Jets that flew morning overflow for UPS. By midmorning, the pilots could refit their jets for passengers, and I chartered them all over the country. From two to 11 aircraft, the company soared. By 2001 I had a charter and maintenance facility at Louisville International Airport...and then 9-11 hit. UPS cut their overflow aircraft of 120 per day to four, from 25 busy employees to no work. By February 2002, we closed to avoid total loss and bankruptcy, and I was back on my own.

Funny how new chapters build on old ones. In college I'd worked around horses at a local racetrack. Now a friend in Canada building low-powered PEMF (pulsed electro-magnetic field) therapy devices for horses asked me to help him sell. "Don't go straight to Churchill Downs," he warned me. "Wait to get to know the racing community." But straight to Churchill Downs I went, where a trainer agreed to break me in. "Come every day and shadow me," he said. "I'll tell you who to talk to, how things work, where to be and when to be there." In a month, I had camaraderie among the horse people and a nice start to business in the horse world—albeit less profitable than aviation, the funeral business, and magazine consulting.

One day I saw a device that appeared to instantly help horses' muscles—a high-powered PEMF not yet ready for prime time. For one thing, it could startle a horse, and no one wants to share a stall with a startled horse.

Maybe two years later, in Atlanta, a woman demonstrated a cool PEMF device on horses that looked stronger and easier to use. Twenty-four hours later a friend in California who worked with horses called to describe a similar machine. And then my wife and I attended a conference in Orlando. A recent fall had left her hobbling with three herniated discs, constant pain, limited mobility—and nothing seemed to help. Not medications, not chiropractors or massage…not until a manufacturer at the conference asked for a volunteer to help demonstrate a high-powered PEMF device for humans. When my wife raised her hand, our future rose with it: After eight minutes of treatment, she stood with total mobility, pain-free.

The price tag on the PEMF was $20,000, and as we left the conference that day, my wife turned to me and asked what I thought of it. It's outstanding, I said innocently, and she smiled. "Great," she said, "because I just bought us one on time."

What I haven't said so far is that we'd just lost our son—28-years-old—and like me he ran hard and played hard. He also had high blood pressure and an undiagnosed heart condition. From time to time you hear about this among athletes; one day the heart just stops, and that happened to our son. In our family's grief, his brother developed a drug problem—and had the same heart issue. (At age 29, he got a defibrillator, and he's now 10 years clean.)

The point is that a year after my son's death, in an emotional spiral, and with $50 in our pockets, my wife and I launched a new business providing high-powered PEMF services, not to get rich but to eat. For the first six months I had the manufacturer effect changes to make it more user friendly. I didn't patent the ideas, but no matter, because today our MagnaWave business tallies $20 million a year, growing by 20 percent a year.

When our son died, my wife and I had both wanted to give up. We took antidepressants, and I drank heavily. Seeing my instability, one wholesaler we'd long worked with released me from our contract, and I reeled. But the doer in me kept doing, and like other hard things in life, what hurt me would ultimately free me. My wife and I would build our business with the help of our remaining children. Struggling with depression and the possibility of addiction, the lot of us limped to the starting line.

Now the sweetheart who got me through college got me through grief and into a new business. Together we kept doing, and from a deficit, our business grew to $100,000 a year. Then $500,000. Then $700,000, where it plateaued. We were traveling full time, working constantly, in an RV...all sales and service on a one-on-one basis. That's when a friend suggested digital marketing, and from a team of four—my wife and me and our son and daughter, a former local TV producer—we became today's business with 62 employees, hiring daily. My daughter, our company president, recently closed on a 35,000-square-foot new headquarters.

MagnaWave today is used about 60 percent veterinary/equine, 40 percent human. Four devices are about to have FDA clearance to go to doctors and hospitals. We're cleared in Australia, the EU, and England, and 120 countries, to sell and ship for veterinarian and human purposes.

A happy new chapter comes with a call to use it to help others. From our years together in business, my wife and I know the good life of homes on wheels, going everywhere, meeting people from everywhere. Recently in Florida we parked near a former prominent retailer and successful politician. A year before, a man broke into this man's house, shot him, threatened his wife, and killed his daughter. The night we met was the anniversary of the murder, and our new friend wanted to die. We know something about loss and death; the three of us talked into the night.

Another time two young men, partners in their early 40s, told us about their unusual business helping animals. Their social media posts have millions of followers. By the evening's end they said, "We didn't come for a coaching session, but you've given us direction." (Often enough, the value of advice is in who gives it. My pricey consultant may say just what my wife says, but somehow an objective third party carries weight.)

Ninety-five percent of couples who lose a child lose their marriages also. My wife and I are still together, the reason for much of today's sanity. Our business travel kept us close in proximity, and as partners we are talkers. From our first date in high school, we agreed to turn off the car radio and talk. When people rode with us, the radio stayed off and we all talked. We have talked through deaths, unhappiness, addictions, and problems because good marriages have hard things. With every new start, we've talked. Under the banner of a common goal, our individual skills keep us close: She talks to people; I talk to horses.

What has life taught me? To play the hand I'm dealt; where I fall short, to develop skills to go around it; that what we learn just to survive, is just what we need to thrive.

God bless the power to overcome. In facing what we can't do, a new world opens to all we can do.

About Pat

Pat Ziemer is the owner of Magna Wave PEMF and Aura Wellness. Pat has been working full time with PEMF since 2002. The company's therapy devices are used extensively on racehorses, performance horses, and professional athletes. Several recent Kentucky Derby winners and numerous world champions in many horse disciplines utilize the therapy regularly. Many NFL, MLB NBA, NHL, MLS teams utilize Magna Wave Therapy.

In 2007, Pat began working with high powered PEMF devices. He branded the devices as Magna Wave and hit the road marketing the Magna Wave brand. Since 2007 the company has placed over 4000 Magna Wave devices into the market for private and professional use.

In 2019 he began the process of having his devices cleared by the FDA and CE marked for international distribution. One device is now registered with the FDA and three more are on course for FDA 510(k) clearance by the third quarter of 2023.

Magna Wave and Aura Wellness now services the human, small animal, and equine markets.

To learn more about Magna Wave visit:

- www.MagnaWavePEMF.com

CHAPTER 4

WHAT BEN SAID

BY RICK BARNETT

On paper, Ben's career was over before it started, but we place people, not resumes, and I gave him the interview.

Sure enough, he was new to the field. And sure as heck he had no experience in or around the kind of high-tech device our client company sold and installed. But viability is more than experience. The three markers we screen for—a strong moral compass, the ability to learn, and high energy—could handily trump previous jobs or a gold-star education.

On the Rep-Lite vocational exam, Ben was check, check, and check, starting with his brutal honesty about himself and where he was in his career. He spoke naturally and often of wanting to do the right thing, and he was hungry, motivated. I could tell because in minutes he was leading the conversation. As for energy, every five minutes he was trying to close the deal.

Thinking back to that interview makes me smile. My corporate client Jamie, for at least two other chapters in my life, had been my work associate, so we had trust. "You're not gonna like this guy's resume or his experience," I emailed her. "But I want you to interview him and take a chance on him."

My company, Rep-Lite, is not normal. A normal placement agency interviews job candidates and hands them off to potential employers. Rep-Lite hands off no one. We interview the candidates, hire them ourselves, and then embed them with their target employers for 12 months of on-the-job learning. At the end of the trial year the employer has hard data for an informed decision on whether to commit to a hire. For the record, 97 percent of our placements are hired, but on that rare occasion that the candidate is a no-fit, Rep-Lite finds and installs a new candidate at zero cost to the client company.

In this case, Jamie interviewed Ben and then picked up her cell and called me. "You're right," she said. "Nice guy but doesn't qualify. Not what we're looking for. But if you put your name on it, I'll give him a shot."

"I put my name on him," I said.

"Then send him down," she said, and by down she meant Florida. Before even a day of employment, on my word, she'd relocate our high-risk candidate to a new state.

Fast-forward two, maybe three years and Ben is running the state of Florida for Jamie's company. Three promotions in, his income is in the high six figures, a bit of intel that came to me about the same time as his 'thank you' message, which someone else will have to erase after I die because I will never delete it.

"Obviously you've changed the trajectory of our entire lives," Ben says in that 2019 voicemail to me and my associates, and it still makes my throat tighten. "From the depths of our hearts we love what you do and give thanks to God for you."

So that's what Rep-Lite does—what *we* get to do—and the kind of feedback that comes to us in emails, texts, thank-you notes, voicemails. And how's that for a day at the office? When my buddies call and ask me what I'm doing, I say, "Changing lives."

MY STORY

I'm a Christian first, a husband and father second, a businessman third. God-family-work is a good order, but it's the work piece I could never seem to fully land. My wife would tell you I'm a Moses, a desert wanderer for 40 years before I found or founded my purpose. Though given what I've gained from across the job market, I think also of J.R.R. Tolkien's saying, "Not all who wander are lost."

In North Carolina, I grew up on a farm in a rural worldview so fixed I could recite my future in 15 words: "Finish your classes, work at a plant for 30 years, and retire with a pension." Saying it now it brings back the claustrophobia I felt as a boy. Factory work didn't appear in even my first hundred choices.

My first choice was to provide for my family doing something I loved. In late high school that would have been baseball or running my own business. I'm right-handed, but thanks to Dad I learned to pitch left-handed. My fastball was 83-84 mph: not speedy but full of junk. I could move it all over the plate, just not enough to get to the pros. As for self-employment, besides the farm work, I maintained a side hustle selling anything from night-crawlers to fishermen, lawn mowing all over the county (once I could drive)...or mobile car washes from the trailer on my truck.

My associate degree was the first college education in our family, self-funded in a work/study program of mostly all work or study. Just as I came up for air, ready to look into bachelor's programs, some buddies swung by for me on their way to an army recruiter. No military for me, I said. Absolutely not. And then we were in Asheville, North Carolina in an army recruiting office, and I was hearing about the GI Bill. And I signed up, served in Special Forces, and redeemed my honorable discharge at the University of Hawaii, at the time offering double value on the GI Bill.

After college, I went into insurance sales like Dad, making more money than a guy knew a human could make until my territories clashed with Dad's, and my interest waned. Back I went for a degree in surgical assisting—as far away as I could get, I remember thinking, from airborne infantry—and from there I ran a hospital's minimally invasive surgery department: hiring, managing, training, steering operations.

One of my first suppliers at the hospital was Stryker medical technology. The Stryker rep studied my department, and after a while he approached me. "Your work here's phenomenal," he said. "Could you grow this kind of thing across the country?"

Just call me employee number one of a Stryker employee-and-training sales division that, 15 years later, comprised 800 people—where I met my wife—overseeing territories across the USA.

And call the Barnetts flexible, because by 2007, my wife and I and the first two of our eventual three kids were leaving the Carolinas for Atlanta, where Intuitive Surgical's global VP of sales wanted me to build its junior sales force, which I did. And just as at Stryker, what we pulled together more than worked. It soared—meeting all key performance indicators and often spilling over...and triggering something in the night-crawler, lawn-mowing, car-washing section of my mind.

"Why not offer this format to companies at large?" I reasoned, and in 2013 Rep-Lite opened for business.

"Rep-Lite?" you say. At the time several med-tech companies were making noises about a 'rep-less' movement—no salespeople—to lower cost-per-unit prices. My thoughts then and now are that rep-less is crazy and will never work. So bypassing rep-less, we called our company Rep-Lite.

And the rep-less idea fell away, as expected, and the Rep-Lite story is still being written.

In a nutshell, Rep-Lite lowers corporate risk and lifts employee prospects. On behalf of our client companies, we find and prepare fresh talent and pay that talent to learn on the job for a year, at which point the client company may choose to hire a dynamo fully trained for its work.

Repeat: All the risk is ours. Because of how we do it, medical corporations, especially medical technologies, where training is everything, snag some of their best employees—and some of their happiest. The job candidate who can apply herself or himself, learn on the go, and integrate into a team, will end a 12-month trial with new skills, new friends, a new employer, and bold new horizons.

By our 11th year, more than 7,000 interviews have helped more than 5,000 people 'get to' learn, 'get to' make a living, and 'get to' make a difference. The candidates who get to the 'get-to,' will have told us who they are in interviews that separate the "How much will I make?" and "How much do I have to do?" candidates from the ones asking, "How can I make a difference?" and "What will I learn?"

The right candidate gets to make a living *and* a difference. As an interviewee, that candidate is honest about where he's been and where she wants to go. He or she is upfront about career struggles because sales trainees only grow great through candor and truth. Like lighting fireworks, we get to match real qualities with the right opportunity, stand back, and BOOM: The client has a dynamite new employee...the employee has a position with a lifetime of payoff...and we have a whole lot of satisfaction.

Does this work that I love provide for my family? Yes, and we're blessed, but again, what makes Rep-Lite different is that it makes a difference in the companies and lives we serve. Recruiters are out there. Staffing agencies abound. But nowhere else, *nowhere else* do they come together. To companies new to the idea, the Rep-Lite idea may take some selling, but to companies who know us the payoff is low risk and obvious.

My greatest satisfaction isn't a paycheck or my influence as an owner and operator. Rep-Lite satisfaction is meeting someone eager to grow, training that person in the context of a company, and two years later, getting the 'You-changed-my-life' text or email.

Companies need more than previous experience., they need 'want-to'. Between jobs, or looking for jobs, people need more than an interview. They need someone to step in with, "I see more in you than you see in yourself. Let me go to bat for you."

Ben had all the parts. I got to help assemble, add fuel, and attend the launch. And the thing is, he's one of hundreds and hundreds and hundreds.

How did I get to my first-choice career? Through love. What Ben said.

About Rick

Rick Barnett has held many senior level executive positions within the medical device arena. He is a performance-driven sales leadership executive with expertise in building client relationships, developing and executing winning sales strategies, and the selection and development of top-talented teams.

Rick Barnett is recognized as a leader with a reputation for advancing successful business development campaigns, leveraging core strengths, and capitalizing on solid client relationships.

He holds a bachelor's degree in Health Services Administration from the University of Hawaii. His background includes building businesses with companies like Stryker and Intuitive Surgical over the past 25 years.

Rick is a visionary who commonly recognizes "outside the box" opportunities while driving the current business to surpass established goals, which has allowed him to function in a consulting capacity for several top industry leaders.

He currently serves as Founder of Rep-Lite and is responsible for spearheading a strategic development process that allows manufacturers to experience maximized potential with limited resources. He has initiated and instituted this process to allow exponential growth within the divisions that it was applied.

One client said of Rep-Lite:
"Rep-Lite has been an invaluable partner to Outset during high-growth commercial scale. There was never an ask too daunting or a timeline too ambitious for Rep-Lite. They moved with us, and for us, every step along the way. I credit Rep-Lite not only with helping us scale quickly and cost efficiently, but also with allowing us to experiment, iterate and refine. They get the big picture, the small details and everything in between." - Leslie Trigg, CEO

Rick Barnett has a proven track record of over 30 years of achieving or surpassing planned goals in every position. When Rick isn't pioneering at

Rep-Lite, he is a known speaker and coach who enjoys giving back to his community in Atlanta, Georgia.

Learn more at:

- www.rep-lite.com

CHAPTER 5

I NEVER EXPECTED TO BE DR. TERI

BY DR. TERI ROUSE

Nothing is impossible. The word itself says 'I'm possible.'
~ Audrey Hepburn

I wasn't always Dr. Teri. For much of my life, 'doctor' next to my name would never have occurred to me.

School tested my patience. Reading bored me; math was my nemesis. Playing in the garden, hiking around the lake, plucking cattails from the mud—anything outside—those were my things, and my parents knew it. They saw me struggle in my classes, but because they knew me they saw past my struggles.

"You'll do great things," they'd tell me. "You're capable, smart, and beautiful."

In time, I married my college sweetheart, but instead of a happy new chapter, my world slowly ripped apart. At first it was just that every decision or choice I made was wrong. Then came the condemnation: "You're stupid! Don't eat that. *You're fat!*"

Before long I stopped making decisions altogether.

When our daughter was born, all hell broke loose. "Make that baby stop crying!" "Toys are all over the place!" "Cut up her food better or she's going to choke!" Translated: *Who do you think you are, you worthless mother.* My husband would threaten to take our daughter and disappear into the woods.

…And I took it. I took all of it.

And one day something happened; I'm not sure I can say what it was. What I know is that in the way the Grinch's heart grew by three sizes, my heart expanded to the point that my mouth said, "No more!"

> *The journey of a thousand miles begins with a single step.*
> ~ Lao Tzu

I was a shell of my old self. 'Dr. Teri' still wasn't a thought in my head.

To set an example for my daughter, and for our safety, I left my toxic marriage to find security with my parents. In a few months, a childhood friend offered me the house next door. More hurdles remained. My job paid poorly; child support was a trickle because getting out had been more important to me than getting out with money. That first winter, I kept the thermostat below 55 degrees for fear I couldn't pay the heating bills. Likewise, I lived in fear of my ex-husband's threats. Kristen and I slept under piles of blankets. We ate cheap hotdogs, PB&J, and canned soup. We'd go next door to my parent's to watch TV, warm up, and accept a "real meal" when mom invited us.

If my parents had known the depths of our struggles, they would have lost their minds. But even then, a pathway was opening. Even then, my impossible was becoming my "I'm possible."

> *Nothing in this world can take the place of persistence. Persistence and determination alone are omnipotent.*
> ~ Calvin Coolidge

I still wasn't Dr. Teri, but before I knew it, I was on a new journey.

I remarried and we bought a house, moving in my preteen daughter and his teenage son. Matthew, now our son, was a full-blown teenager with all that implies. My daughter, for her part, struggled to adjust to the divorce and remarriage, to having an older brother, to the new house, and to the guilt feelings that came with leaving her dad. All of it I carried, or tried to carry, on my Superwoman cape.

I wasn't 'Dr. Teri' yet, but a crack in the wall was letting in light.

> *Time does not change us, it unfolds us.*
> ~ Max Frisch

Unfold it did—or you could say the clean slate my husband and I hoped for lasted all of 60 seconds.

Matthew's new start quickly devolved into school detentions and suspensions. He was repeatedly caught skipping class and smoking on the school bus. Once he stole a scale from the chemistry lab. Our house became a battleground with skirmishes over homework and chores. Kristen would ride the bus home from school and beeline for her room, emerging only for dinner. Neither child had friends over. Dr. Fred and I scratched our heads and wrung our hands, desperate for solutions, grasping for help. The school offered only more detentions and more and longer suspensions. Family and friends offered mostly harsh comments, but I beat them to the criticism. "Bad mother!" ran in my head on an infinity loop.

Our exchanges with Matthew could explode with such a light trigger that we fell off guest lists to parties and BBQs. We were shunned. Increasingly isolated at home. The fights with Matthew, the school, and each other left us emotionally depleted.

I still wasn't 'Dr. Teri'... .

> *Winners never quit, and quitters never win.*
> *~ Vince Lombardi*

Three months before his graduation, Matthew left school. The system failed him and us, yes, but that couldn't touch the shame, the despair, the fear, the anger, the frustration that we heaped on our parenting.

From those depths, from that pain, my mission began to form to help other parents never have to know *our* depths of isolation, chaos, and heartache. In our struggles, failures, and triumphs, we were in training unawares to help other parents find peace, learn to communicate, take joy in each other, and create lifetime memories. The mission coming together on this battlefield would send me to school for a doctorate.

First, however, I had to overcome myself. I believed I was stupid, and I can tell you where I was the day the despair in me won and my husband, Fred, looked at me as if I had six heads. "Are you out of your damn mind?" he said incredulously. "Of course you can do this, you should do this, and you will."

Period.

> *You are braver than you believe, stronger than you seem,*
> *and smarter than you think.*
> *~ A.A. Milne, "Winnie the Pooh"*

Off I went in my big girl pants to a doctoral program in special education—the oldest student in the cohort by 15 years— or should I say, old enough and wounded enough to refuse to quit. Even hard circumstances served me. In my second year of studies, a herniated disk requiring back surgery made it difficult for me to walk. But that was the year, though math is my nemesis, that I took and survived statistics. Walking or not, I studied, I wrote, I worked projects, created graphs, tackled studies, and wrote more. And rewrote. And rewrote again. My life had become the practicum, the education, and a launch pad. I consumed everything possible about special education, behavior, and positive behavior support.

And a day came when my name came with a "Doctor." Dr. Teri... Dr. Mommy Teri...Dr. Mommy Teri Rouse.

Take that, naysayers.

> *It is easier to build strong children than to repair broken men.*
> *~ Frederick Douglass*

Kristen grew into the strong and independent woman she is today. Matthew is cut off from us. Across ten years and two *very different* outcomes, I identified, practiced, and refined a growing body of reasonable, manageable wisdom for parents: how to help their children gain successful independent lives *and* remain attached. From my own experience and from intense study under experts, I began to assemble the toolbox to help *all* parents, not just those in crisis—tools both practical and preventive—to build peace, communicate better, take joy in one another, and create a lifetime of memories.

My mission now is for all families to have what our family needed so badly—ways to regain power, to create calm, to increase communication, to diminish the chaos—in safe spaces free of judgment.

I share those tools now in classes, in counsel, and in my writing—in sometimes deceptively simple concepts like these, to help children build healthy independence:

Tip #1:   Give positive attention.

Catch your children being good and praise them for it. Affirming desirable behavior says you pay attention and salute good behavior.

NEWSFLASH: The words 'good job' or 'thanks' are nice but vague. To get more of a certain behavior, be *literal*: "Thank you for putting your laundry in the hamper." "You did a great job raking the leaves." (How would you like your boss at work to praise you?)

Tip #2:   Give your kids some control in decision-making.

In a kid's eyes, adults have all the control, and in a sense we do control choices and decisions—which we've come to from a lifetime of mistakes and feedback.

As a child, you may have decided what foods you'd eat or avoid. In your teens, you made choices regarding college and work. Then came big-life decisions about marriage and where to live (some outcomes better than others). A person starts small, hits walls, learns from experience—and builds her or his decision-making muscles. Help your kids build those muscles with low-risk ways to consider what they want and know against outcomes.

But, you ask, what if I'm uncomfortable handing off decisions to my child(ren)?

Remember that the more that little people can master small choices, the better they grow into the bigger choices. The sooner they face decisions, however small, the faster they mature in making choices. You're not handing away all control over all things, just enough control over a few things.

Tip # 3:   Help Your Kids Understand and Accept Consequences

A consequence is a neutral result, something neither bad nor good. Kids who finish their chores have time for something they want to do. That's a good consequence. Kids who ignore their chores have other consequences.

Even as adults we learn consequences when we stay out late, for instance, and oversleep and miss an important meeting.

Empowering our children to choose clothes or breakfast foods helps them master in a small way what will soon come to them in a big way. Set a few guidelines: no Spiderman costume at school, for example. And narrow the breakfast choices to, say, bacon & eggs or cereal.

NEWSFLASH: Once your child chooses, stick to it. No parental flip-flops. Unbending consequences teach children that they can't change their minds at will. The big bad world doesn't work that way, and neither should parents.

To help your children make decisions, teach them to ask:

- What will result from my choice?
- Who else will it affect?
- Most important, can I accept and live with the outcome?

Tip #4: Equip your kids with self-care, boundaries, expectations, and routines.

All kids—repeat, *all*—need both consistency and flexibility. The behavior trifecta—boundaries, expectations, and a set schedule—helps kids (and the adults over them) keep their behaviors in check. Flexibility allows for every day's inevitable surprises.

Routine and flexibility. Not so flexible that kids set the schedule, but a day of MUST DO's that also allows for WANT TO's. When I taught children with severe behavior issues, checking off the MUST DO's gave students some control to pursue the WANT TO's.

MUST DOs may be to make the bed, feed the dog, get ready for school. WANT TO's—non-essential and fun—might be a puzzle, a book, play in the yard. In tackling the MUST DO's to choose among the WANT TO's, a child controls both consequences and rewards.

NEWSFLASH: Letting a child choose a WANT TO willy-nilly is a recipe for disaster. *You create that list.*

NEWSFLASH TWO: The more a child experiences both consistency of life *and* flexibility to change as needed, the lower his or her anxiety and the greater the emotional control.

One of our children grew up to take on a successful adult life. One cut us off. Life comes with no guarantees. Our job is to take on the struggles, the challenges, the fear…and to seek wisdom, build community, and navigate the outcomes.

Change is possible—that's the point—and every family is worth the fight and the grace. I never expected to be Dr. Teri, but I am: wounded, wiser, helping other families become families, truly, in the best sense of the word.

If you change nothing, nothing changes.
~ Dr. Joyce Brothers

About Dr. Teri

Dr. Teri Rouse, more often called Dr. Teri by friends, family, students and clients, is a wife, mother, certified autism specialist, behavior and early interventionist, educational coach and consultant, multiple best-selling author, creator of Snuggle Bunny Story Time, and a speaker. However, most importantly, she is a woman who cares passionately for the wellbeing of children and their families, and she has made it her mission to help families navigate through the chaos and create peace and tranquility in their homes.

She has spent over 22 years in classrooms as a Special Education Teacher, Behavioral Specialist, Early Interventionist, Autism Specialist, and Applied Behavior Analyst. Not only did Dr. Teri work in classrooms, but she has spent the last 17 years teaching teachers how to teach at Chestnut Hill College, Widener University and Penn State. In 2016, she decided to work with private clients and founded KIDS: Interventions & Direct Services – where she is the Managing Director.

Because of her extensive classroom experiences and her personal experiences as a parent/step-parent of a child with significant behavioral issues, she has written a book, *Untamed Chaos: a Guide to Improving Communication, Resolving Conflict, and Restoring Peace in Your Home*. She has also created several programs to help families create peace and tranquility in their homes so they can live the life they so desire.

Dr. Teri is a member of the National Academy of Best-Selling Authors and the Recipient of multiple QUILLY Awards. Her books include *Cracking the Code to Success* and *Success*. She also authored *Julian's Gift* – a children's book inspired from her over 22 years in the Pre-K to 8th grade classrooms.

She travels the globe to give presentations at conferences for teachers, school administrators, organizations and conventions such as the American Horticultural Therapy Association and the Division of International Special Education & Services. Dr. Teri is involved with Division of International Special Education & Services, The Council for Exceptional Children (CEC), Light it Up Blue for Autism, Autism Speaks, Lily's Hope Foundation and Uthando, South Africa.

To connect with Dr. Teri and learn more about her work, including how to get involved with Snuggle Bunny Book Club and other programs, please visit:

- http://drterirouse.com
- https://www.facebook.com/profile.php?id=100066649597482
- https://www.facebook.com/teri.wiedemanrouse
- https://www.instagram.com/dr_teri_rouse/

Join her FB group: KIDS Power Positive Transformations

CHAPTER 6

A LOVE STORY

BY PATTI MAGAN

One day in my junior year of college I gave up.

I'd loved the theater for every chance it gave me to be anyone but me. Growing up in my family had been hard, and to my thinking I had no value. At Rutgers' Mason Gross School of the Arts, I majored in theater, drawn to the stories with happy endings.

School I paid for by working as a deejay, sleeping into the day, running tunes at night. I drank, smoked pot, flirted…I made a great living. Except for the income, I was a standard college kid. One spring semester I auditioned to join an ensemble theater group affiliated with the school, and I got in, to my amazement. We performed all over—up and down the East Coast and three weeks in Scotland at the Edinburgh Theatre Festival. On the last night of the tour, I was raped.

How I got back to my hotel room that night is a blur. I remember turning on the shower and sitting on the tile floor, crying harder than I knew a body could cry. Then I was under the covers, still crying. sobbing. I couldn't stop. When the sun came up, I started for the bus that was taking us home, but the stage manager saw me and put me in her car. She helped me call the police and get tested for STDs and pregnancy, both negative.

After that, all I could do was cry or sleep, sleep or cry. If I was nobody before, now I was nothing. I dropped out of college, unable to get out of bed. Three weeks after the rape, alone in my studio apartment, I stared at the prescription bottle with the meds to slow my heart. The bottle was full, recently refilled, and I said out loud, "I'm done." I went into the kitchen, poured myself a glass of water, downed the bottle's entire contents, and waited to die.

Next thing I'm in a hospital bed, angry as a hornet, looking up at my boyfriend, who had found me with the empty prescription bottle and called an ambulance.

Psychotherapy helped a lot. I went back to deejay work and enrolled in karate training. For a while I worked at the karate school, which led to work in the fitness industry, which led to work with Gary Patti, who's also in this book, who had a lot to say to me about God.

Gary called God his 'heavenly father,' which made no sense to me. His gym was booming; he held leadership meetings where the God subject regularly came up. In business conversations or reviewing numbers he'd say God blessed the work. He was forever telling me how much God loves me.

He'd say God cares for every detail in our lives, and that if I pray, God will help me. Prayer is talk, he'd say. You just talk to God. And I'd think he was crazy, but I'd try it. He gave me a bible and invited me to church. "An hour out of your week," he'd say. "What have you got to lose?"

After a year of this kind of warm up, one Sunday morning I got dressed and went to church with Gary, who mentioned in passing that the service might strike me as a little different. Sure enough, we walked in not to the organ strains of someone's grandmother at a massive keyboard, but to the rock beat of a musical trio in dark suits, looking for all the world like ZZ Top. Backed by guitars and drums, the vocalists sang, and I wept, and that's where my love story begins. Not immediately, not consistently—not consistently for a long time—but eventually and, one day fully, I was with God, and the more I opened myself to Him the more inclined I was to give up again, this time not to end the pain but to sink into trust.

However often I might or might not make it to church, God showed up for me. In a year or two I was married and pregnant, and at 32 weeks with Christina I had some kind of flu. I spent a day in bed; the baby was strangely still, but I let it slide. What I'm about to tell you now may sound flakey, but I'll swear on anything that in the middle of the night an angel said to me, "Your daughter is very, very ill. You need to get to a hospital." My husband was out of town; my obstetrician arranged to meet me at her office. Several hurried tests, more doctors, and still no movement from the baby, and the same night as the angel's warning, I was induced. Christina spent ten days in NICU, and last year my brilliant daughter collected her diploma at NYU and headed to grad school.

A few years later, in the last days of my marriage, I was pregnant with Olivia, now my 19-year-old in school in Boca Raton, when my body interpreted the fetus as a foreign invader and tried to knock it out with antibodies. The treatment for such cases didn't work, meaning my body was still attacking the baby. "If she survives the pregnancy," my doctor informed me, "she'll probably need a full blood transfusion."

What! If she survives? My church had Friday-night renewal services, and I showed up sobbing. A woman—a second mother to me—saw me, brought five or six women to me, and told them my story. Each woman put a hand on me and began to pray, and I was praying. "God, God, God...*save my baby, save my baby*" ...and then my body was in tumult. The baby was spinning, tumbling, kicking, practicing leaps and dismounts for future glory. The words came to my mind, "It is finished. All is well," and Olivia my gold-medal gymnast came into the world early and perfect.

Two babies and no husband may seem desperate, but my desperate days were past. Whatever came, I was surrounded by prayer and hands-on help. When I got a new corporate job out of state, people in my church helped me get my house on the market, even painted the house—the entire house.

I was in. In church. In the bible. In love with God. Engaged with people. Some Sunday mornings I wondered if I should fill a seat in the pew because of the tears and sadness, but those emotions, sitting there with God, came out laced with relief. I believed now that whatever I gave to Him, I could get through.

One day I was in bed reading the Bible when I saw words that described my life. Jeremiah 29:11 became my life scripture: "'For I know the plans I have for you,' says the Lord. 'Plans for good and not for disaster, to give you a future and a hope.'"

Life still throws hardballs; those don't stop. Lately I've moved through the stages, surgeries, decisions, fatigue, and treatments of a breast cancer diagnosis. This minute I'm recovering from a fourth surgery, aware that God turns even the worst of our past to our benefit. At one point in my life I had a diagnosis of PTSD—post-traumatic stress disorder.

A survival skill of people with PTSD is to disassociate, to emotionally detach. In relationships, you don't want to do that, but during the cancer surgeries, again surrounded with prayer, my emotional distance helped me endure what was happening.

So two things are true. One, growing up in my family had its difficulties, and two, I was reborn into a far bigger family that embraces my parents too. We are all forgiven, all made new by love. It's not that I never gave up. I did. In despair, I gave up and tried to end my life. My love story is that God never gives up on us.

Where can I go from your Spirit? Where can I flee from your presence? If I go up to the heavens, you are there; if I make my bed in the depths, you are there. If I rise on the wings of the dawn, if I settle on the far side of the sea, even there your hand will guide me, your right hand will hold me fast.
Psalm 139: 7-10

About Patti

Patti Magan is a business leader, a survivor of sexual abuse, domestic violence, major career challenges, and breast cancer. She is a proud single mother of two amazing young women—living proof that God turns hard times into riches.

When Patti isn't with her daughters or serving as a Risk Manager for an insurance brokerage (before that as Vice President of a large third-party administrator), she speaks to audiences large and small about The Never-Ending Love she knows firsthand. An encourager by nature, she embodies understanding and hope. To people who are lost and downhearted, Patti says from experience, "God is in the business of transforming painful pasts."

This short chapter is a small part of her story.

Patti Magan lives in New Jersey; since 2007 she's served on her church's Board of Trustees.

To learn more, contact Patti at:

- pattimagan@gmail.com

CHAPTER 7

RISING FROM THE COLD

BY DR. SAM NGUYEN

Saigon is in South Vietnam, where winters are hot, spring is hot, and summer is hotter. One steamy summer day in December 1993 my parents and five siblings and I boarded a plane in Saigon, flew 18 hours to Lincoln, Nebraska, and landed in temperatures 22 degrees below freezing.

Funny what cold can teach person: what shelter is, how to create warmth from what's available, why it matters to see others in the cold and share the safety. Those lessons would forever shape my life.

My father left the plane that night in a thin wrap of aristocracy and arrogance. In Vietnam, he was a 13th-generation doctor in Traditional Chinese Medicine, a descendent of royal physicians. His mother's early death and his father's remarriages had swept him to the margins, but in school he excelled and grew haughty. Away from home he saved lives; at home, he was cruelty in human form, drinking his days away, destroying his family by degrees.

His marriage to my mother was arranged, and in the way he crushed life, she gave it. She was a nurse, a midwife who'd owned a clinic delivering many children of Vietnamese women and

American soldiers. One orphan of a Black American father and a Vietnamese mother became our brother, eventually opening our passage to the United States.

I will forever remember our first night at the Lincoln airport, chilled to the bone and disoriented. Someone drove us to a house in the country with the telephone service still disconnected and a faulty heating system. Everything was foreign. To warm ourselves, we tried lying between the mattress and box springs. At 3:30 a.m. our sponsor, Mr. Lucas, came to our door, and desperately I pantomimed our plight—shaking and rubbing my arms. He drove back to his house an hour away and returned with our first-ever heater and blankets.

The next week we were moved in town to a small house more than a hundred years old and infested with roaches. Our adjustments were just beginning. In Vietnam, parents and teachers were respected, television coverage was limited, much of the country was rural, and ethnicities were rare. My brother was Black, but except for athletes in Olympic games, our media showed us nothing of Black lives. That first morning in Lincoln, staring through ice-frosted windows we saw a Black schoolgirl, her hair braided dramatically to stand a foot from her head. Was that normal? The next day her hair had changed, and she had a cigarette. My God, she smoked? Other kids shocked us with their painted fingernails.

In our new life of scarcity, we learned to make do or improvise. Our old car had a heater, but no air conditioner except for holes in the floor. I lost my shoes once through the holes on the way to church. Our house had one bathroom, and every morning the toilet stopped up. To shower we'd carry water by bucket to the old tub. Our mattresses I spread out in the small house's living area until my father's fits drove us to a cramped bedroom, where he'd open the door to scream at us. We were all nobodies, he'd shout, destined to be hoods and prostitutes. His profanities landed on us like rotting garbage, tempting us to see garbage in ourselves.

For our mother he used every foul name possible, grabbing her hair to throw her into the snow. And yet she was strong-minded. Calling the police would only cause more problems, she'd say, and some days I saw no reason to live. Other days my mother would pull us aside to insist, "This is my life, but not yours. If you want to do something, I will help you." She was everything to me.

My mother gave birth to 11 children—I'm number seven—and raised 12 more besides. My love of orphans comes from her. Her father was a dean at a French School in Vietnam, open to new ideas, but when he united his lively daughter with my father, he married a modern girl to generations of tradition and pain. How can I describe the suffering in our house? It was physical and psychological, misery on misery for people already doing their best just to survive. Holidays my father would insist that we cook a feast, then we'd sit at the table, and he'd unleash on us. We were fools, he'd say, jokes, an embarrassment—foul and undeserving. Our lives would be worse than nothing. In those years, who needed soup? Our days were filled with tears. In our family pictures, every face looks hopeless.

My first job after school was for an electric-battery company from 3:15 p.m. to midnight. I would have stayed longer, but in the freezing temperatures Dad would call me *loser* and *stupid*. Weekends I steam ironed for a drycleaner, who soon promoted me to wedding gowns. When his tailor left, I sewed on buttons for $2 a shirt. At my school, I scrubbed toilets and floors. In every job, within a week or two I'd be a manager, supervising.

A person can live many stories at once. In my classes I quickly rose to top student. At home, and within myself, I was unsure who to be or whether to live or die. One day I wrote an assigned essay about my life in America, saying what's normal for an American was another planet to me. Like pizza in the cafeteria: I'd smother it under catsup while Americans stared at me and Asian kids disdained me (though six months later I was their tutor).

In that essay I described the hardships of not knowing. We didn't know how to catch a bus, so we walked the 23 blocks to school. Snow days: What were those? When the town shut down in a cold front, over streets and sidewalks blanketed by the downfall, my brother and I walked the long miles only to find the school locked. We stood outside, blue with cold. A janitor there would mock us to be funny. From inside the warm building she saw us and said, "Why you here?" waving her hand at us as if to say, "Shoo." My brother and I stared at her. We stared at the upside-down world we'd somehow fallen into. About that time, a man pulled up with his son in the car. The family went to our church, and his son said they'd take us home.

In the essay, I described life for kids new to the US with no support, and something struck a chord. Newspaper and television reporters interviewed me. Radio stations called me. I own a television network now; I know the value of a story, a human face, a message…but at the time, I understood nothing.

All I knew was that what was normal to us drew stares and mockery. On our morning walk to school, a few kids would shout: "Good morning, f--- you!" I'd smile back in greeting, and the other kids would burst out laughing. This happened until I learned what the F-word meant and resolved to stand up for myself. The next morning when the kids said it to us, I said, "Thank you. You, too," and the crowd of kids laughed at them.

Incident by incident, job by job, new word by new word, I ascended a staircase. I was determined to climb to the top, even when new circumstances sent me bumping and rolling back to the basement.

For months after our arrival in Lincoln, in our pre-Google and foreign world, everywhere I went I carried a thousand-page English-Vietnamese dictionary. One day I entered a Dollar General Store wanting a bag to carry the book, and I found one but was unsure of its size. Ignorant of exchanges or returns, I placed the book on top of the bag to measure against it, and when I did, the cashier called the police.

Horrified, I stood alone in the store aisle, red-faced and helpless. I wanted to flee, but the woman told me to stay, and there I was when the sirens stopped and flashing lights filled the store. A large policeman came in with a gun on his hip.

In broken English, shaking, I described my actions, and the cashier gave her version. The policeman sent me home, and still trembling, I pushed open the door to leave, promising myself that no one would bully my people if I could help it. Days later, I volunteered at a hospital and schools, helping interpret for fellow refugees.

Soon I was interpeting at the Lincoln Police Department, where I also created a Southeast Asian Youth Club of five members: me as leader and four kids utterly lost, miserable at home, unable to cook, with no idea what to eat, and working to survive. When my father was out, I'd slip them into our roach-ridden basement, which we all did our best to clean. One day someone found a discarded drum set and we bought it home. Another day we found a guitar, and then a keyboard. Before you knew it we had enough noise to make us happy and were playing all the time. The LPD sponsored our Southeast Asian Youth Club—this still moves me—led by the policeman from the Dollar Store.

When he and I met again, he didn't know me, so I reminded him that a Dollar Store lady accused me of stealing, and all he said was, "Oh, yeah. Stupid lady!" The LPD gave us a place to meet, and when we had get-togethers to play music, they looked out for us. From the street, it must have looked like a big event with all the police cars pulled up to the door.

Day by day, I learned to stand up for myself, and to see and defend others like me. From my years on the margins, I could see the children that others overlooked. At first informally, and then officially, my life took shape around getting these children to safety or to a home. If no one else could help, I would do what it took.

Formally, I lead The SAM Foundation—Stable Anchor Manor—giving kids the basics to survive: a person to love them, money to live on, a place to come home to…in the context of their needs. In Vietnam, SAM is an orphanage. In the US, it is what happens around me.

In Texas, for instance, my home became a magnet to CPS kids escaping homes with addiction or abuse; maybe the parents were in jail. Someone was paid to care for these kids, but they would run to my house, and I would take them in. I understood their pain, and compensation was irrelevant.

"I don't want to break laws, but they can stay with me," I'd tell the schools, and slowly their grades rose from failing to B's and C's. The kids would live with me or under my guidance from eighth and ninth grades until age 25. Why? Because human trafficking and drugs intensify at age 18 when kids are tossed out of the system into the deep end. In 2016, our Teen Achieve Scholarship awarded its first funding for college.

It matters to reach kids while they're young. In 2008, I was in Vietnam helping anyone who needed it when a friend, a nun, asked me to visit an orphanage about to close for lack of money. I flew to the region and drove several hours to a mountainside village where I found the orphanage. Inside, children reached for me with their hands and their eyes. Within minutes I was saying, "You're all my kids now." Their parents had died or left them, and they were beautiful and smart. I would provide for their needs—school or anything—to help them live normal lives.

Since 2017, I spend a third of each month in Vietnam, in the meantime using every means—pageants, products, productions, you name it—to embrace these children and lift their futures.

My biography says more about that. In 2015 and again in 2022, Presidents Barak Obama and Joe Biden, respectively, recognized my work, my love, with the President's Volunteer Service.

Some children emigrate to the cold or must flee to it. Some are born into it. Some fall into it through the cracks. My early pain in the US is my gift now to children around the world. The cold years taught me to build fires—to warm others and push back the darkness. There is always more to do, but everything I do, for as many children as I can, is to gather kindling and light the winter sky.

About Dr. Sam

Dr. Sam Nguyen— Dr. Sam—is a distinguished Doctor of Naturopathy, accomplished entrepreneur, television personality, graduate of Harvard Business School and UCLA Anderson's executive programs, and talented musician, singer, and pageant winner. She is most proud of her eight children (two biologicals, six foster), and business and pageantry platforms generating hope and help for those in need.

Dr. Sam Nguyen is high profile in Vietnam and in Vietnamese communities worldwide, known for her outreach, especially for children. Merging business and naturopathy, she pioneers and markets holistic oils and herbal medicines to help patients around the globe, even addressing certain cancers.

Dr. Sam was Ms. National United States Woman of Achievement 2016; Ms. Texas Woman of Achievement 2015; Miss Asia Woman of Achievement International 2014; and Miss Vietnam, University of Lincoln Nebraska 1994—advancing foster care reform, receiving the Community Platform Award and Brad Harper Style awards.

Her humanitarian work is recognized by cities (including Frisco, Texas ~ Sam Nguyen Day; Los Angeles, and Long Beach), groups (for example, Asian American Chamber of Commerce and Viet Nam National University of Economic and Law), and the US Congress. She received 2015 and 2022 President's Volunteer Service Awards from Presidents Barack Obama and Joe Biden, respectively, for Lifetime Achievement – a US president's highest recognition, honoring her more than 4,000 hours of service.

Dr. Sam's charitable work is featured across the media, currently for *Stable Anchor Manor* (S.A.M.) Foundation, established in Texas in 2009 to support and guide homeless, runaway, and at-risk youth. In 2017, she also founded the S.A.M. Foundation in Orange County. The S.A.M Teen Achieve Scholarship, founded in 2016, has awarded its first student college tuition. Dr. Sam supports Helping Hands, One Body Village (against human trafficking), Children's Cancer Hospital in Vietnam, and orphanages in Vietnam. She stays involved with Vietnamese community events such as

Bolsa's annual New Year parade. Besides her family, she loves playing the drums, singing, and remodeling.

CHAPTER 8

THE *ADD* ADVANTAGE

BY DR. FRED ROUSE

My mom was an Italian girl from South Philly, so all her family lived nearby, and we saw each other. Sundays by eleven or noon everyone was at Grandmom's house for dinner at three o'clock. The day was full of exuberant conversation with gestures, hugs, kisses, and shouting. That's my Italian side. Mom was about emotion.

Dad came from German stock, lower middle class, which he worked to rise out of. He was a carpet installer, and he was quiet. In his spare time he became a body builder. When our family moved three doors down to a house on the corner, we dug into the clay basement for him to have a gym. He entered physique contests, but I recall no wins. I regret that I didn't know until a year before he died that he was a medic with a Marine unit in Korea. That tells so much about his story.

My story turns on ADD—attention deficit disorder. 'Disorder' I leave to the medical experts, but 'deficit' I challenge. The stereotype of ADD is someone with all energy and no focus, but there's focus to spare. It's just intense focus on one or two things.

Or let me put it this way. What do Albert Einstein, Michael Jordan, Richard Branson, and John F. Kennedy have in common?

That's right. Scratch any high-level achiever—I've said this for a long time—and you find some level of ADD. Statistically, 7 percent of us have it, but my point is that where focus meets interest, ADD is an asset.

On the other hand, where no interest exists the boredom can move a person with ADD right out the door. I quit high school in my third year. Why go to class when you can read the book? Since my mind also needs structure, I joined the U.S. Coast Guard when I turned 17 to run gun boats in Vietnam. I'd seen my share of John Wayne movies; what I hadn't seen—not outside of a fire hydrant—was much water…and I couldn't swim.

So the Coast Guard was not my Hollywood ending, but for a kid who was all mouth and no brains, it was an education and mental scaffolding. After boot camp taught me to swim the length of an Olympic pool, my first duty station embedded me in structure and challenge: 12 hours on, 12 hours off at a light house in Delaware Bay.

All of it interested me, that's the thing, and I mastered the work.

SEARCH AND RESCUE

In my second year in the Coast Guard, I was trained and assigned to the search-and-rescue station at Cape May: four boats, 40 men, 1,036 rescues a year. At age 18, I knew how to master a structure and find my place in it. I steered my small craft into rough seas, fires, capsizings…and running hours of search patterns for lost boaters.

On my own time, I certified as an EMT technician and volunteered on a local rescue squad. By sea and by land, inside and out, I knew the cardiorespiratory system, and I loved the work. When my four years ended, I re-upped for another year. Now I was overseeing Cape May base maintenance, with military and civilian personnel under me.

Life outside the military rocked my world until I landed at a community college studying respiratory therapy—and took an elective in real estate. I stayed in rescue as an EMT, and with more training became an EMT instructor for NJ State, but the real hook was real estate.

I dropped out of college and drilled into books and specialized classes. True to my ADD focus, I became the smartest real estate broker in Cape May County, graduating from the Realtor Institute (GRI), then taking advanced classes to be a CCIM (Certified Commercial Investment Manager). I was licensed to list, sell, lease commercial, industrial, and residential properties—and make money.

And I did, until the 2008 mortgage collapse, sending me back to school for respiratory therapy. Back in a structured environment, I learned respiratory exhaustively from big picture to details, serving at Cooper University Hospital in urban, level-one trauma and neo-natal units, as well as ICU, CCU, and PedICU. If I had a weak spot, it was on the people side, in the intense emotions of the patients and their families.

I think of myself as a closet romantic—my Italian side, maybe—but like my dad, I am mostly quiet and detached. In the rescue business, that brand of cool is an asset. A person trapped in a burning building isn't praying for someone with social skills.

Medicine is another story. I stayed in respiratory work—in critical care units on peds, med-surg, oncology, and psych—until the emotional side undid me. A patient would stop breathing, and when the resident couldn't intubate, I could. But as a medical crisis abated and the traumatized family came in, I was looking for the exit.

Six years into respiratory therapy, the final straw was pediatric ICU, and I exchanged severely injured kids on breathing machines for home care of older patients on ventilators: house calls, in and out, multiple counties a day. No surprises, no emergencies, I just showed up and got it done…and I stayed for years.

GREED IS NOT GOOD

When I needed more money, I got into financial planning, selling mutual funds, life insurance, and annuities. The selling part I hated. Days I served as a respiratory therapist; nights I was in school to become a Certified Financial Planner—a CFP. This qualified me to do taxes; it was cleaner work in my mind, with more structure and less selling. It also played to my strengths – just master the regulations and make them work for my clients. During that time a year of law school grounded me in black-letter law, which I also loved. The law is literal.

A CFP majors in mutual funds, stocks, and bonds, not commodities. When I took a course to fill that gap, right away I began pulling in more than 300 percent returns. *Phenomenal*, I thought. In and out. Put in a thousand and the leverage hands you thousands more. I bought more books, took more courses, and in two years my $5,000 trading account was at $2 million.

I must be a genius, right? Hold that thought, because I tried to double it and in six months I lost it all. *How?* How could I scorch so much so fast? Answer: Why do new sports stars burn through multimillion dollar contracts? *I didn't understand big money.* More than that, my emotions had surfaced. Where greed meets anxiety, I lost my cool, and I then lost my judgment. Shortly after that, the world crashed around me and I lost my desire to get out of bed.

To pay the bills, I was back working nights and weekends at a long-term ventilator-care facility. Weekdays, I ran a tax-and-business-management office, forever asking myself what happened to that $2 million. I read volumes on trading. I took courses. I followed the gurus. Much of what I read was trash, but nothing else had ever brought that much money that fast.

And I stuck with studying commodities, and 10 years later I had more than an answer—I had a system, and that system had structure—ADD guardrails.

It took a loud alarm to awaken me to the deadly mix in my life of emotion and judgment, and for me to understand how my ADD can either serve me or sabotage the works. I'd never been diagnosed with it, by the way. My new wife, a former Special Ed teacher, first pointed it out to me. With that information, I could see how ADD drew me to certain kinds of work: detailed and high stakes, crowning competence over emotion…work where all I had to be was an expert.

By the end of ten years of research and $350,000 of testing, I had mastered commodities my way: detached, repetitive, and grounded in reason. Simple and sure. Let other CFPs get their clients 8 or 12 percent all over the board. My students would bring in triple-digit returns by trading just two commodities—any two—in one structured system…over and over and over… no changes.

STILL IN A BOAT

I'll say it again. A highly successful person either has more than a touch of ADD or benefits from someone who does. People like me are atypical and individualistic, problem-solvers, and determined. We tend not to work for other people or for salaries. We tend to inhale information and exhale structure.

I'm still in the rescue business. By 'rescue,' I mean I show people how to get their finances under control and get back above the water line. I show them how to retire sooner, free of worry about inflation, taxes, stock-market crashes or having to work into their 80s.

Most of the students in my commodities courses come to me in leaky financial boats or gasping for air. Most are in their late fifties or early sixties, ranging from blue-collar tradespeople to professionals in law and medicine. The average have $50,000 to $350,000 in savings. The luckiest have up to $1.6 million saved.

When late-career clients want to fix their futures, most financial people will tell them they're already sunk—or further weight their crafts with mutual funds, life insurance, and annuities.

That's a thing about getting older. You turn around, and what looks like a trail of random jobs forms a path to who you're made to be. My mom would recognize the crowds in my life. My dad would recognize the introversion that my wife has helped me name.

By any label, I'm still helping people breathe.

About Dr. Fred

Dr. Fred Rouse, aka 'The REAL Money Doctor', is an award-winning and best-selling author of multiple books. He is a retired certified financial planner and the nation's leading authority on short-window retirement planning.

Near the end of the Vietnam War, he served five years in the US Coast Guard running small boats for search-and-rescue. He spent ten years as a Registered Respiratory Therapist (RRT), starting in a small community hospital and ending up at a large inner-city university teaching hospital working the ICU, CCU, Pediatric ICU, Level 1 Trauma, and Level 1 NICU. On the side, he founded a business in financial services, eventually earning his credential as a Certified Financial Planner—which he held for the last 28 of his 40 years in financial services before he retired.

In his early days, Dr. Rouse turned a $5,000 account into $2 million dollars in two years. Attempting to double that, he lost it all in six months. To pay the bills, he went back to nights and weekends as an RRT, while weekdays building his tax and business advisory service by serving individuals and small businesses with 0-6 employees.

Ten years and $350,000 later, he had researched, developed, tested, and retested a financial system freeing him to retire. The stock market crash in 2008 failed to dent his system's predictable cash flow results, which consistently outperformed the markets. Two years more and the system was a course for his clients, men and women desperately needing predictable cash flow for the option to retire sooner—or at all.

Short Window Retirement Planning is the only system exclusively for the unique needs of people that want Faster Financial Independence and to get a jump start on their retirement.

Now in his retirement, Dr. Rouse wants to help others get, protect, and enjoy their money, life, and retirement. His small program shows others how to enjoy retirement sooner regardless of world events, independent of stock market ups and downs.

Dr. Rouse has been quoted in *The Wall Street Journal, FORBES, Newsweek, Inc Magazine,* and more. His work has been seen on ABC, NBC, CBS, Fox, CNBC networks and on other TV and cable outlets.

Dr Fred, his wife Dr Teri, and their dog Gus-Gus split their time between their home in the Philadelphia suburbs and their shore house on the bay in southern Delaware.

Learn more at:

- https://DrRouseNow.com/
- https://DrFredRouse.com/

CHAPTER 9

UNBREAKABLE HOPE

BY GARY PATTI

A *typical human is born with 270 bones that will fuse into somewhere from 206 to 213 bones. The numbers vary because humans may have varied numbers of ribs, vertebrae, and digits.*

I came into this world in 1957, the third and youngest of three sons. When I was two weeks old a bone broke—my femur or 'thigh' bone—and for no apparent reason. I was still a baby in my parents' arms. I doubt the doctor suspected foul play. He knew my family. He'd delivered my two healthy brothers. But 14 days later, I was back in with my other femur broken, and this time there was a diagnosis: osteogenesis imperfecta, OI, a genetic condition also known as 'brittle bone disease,' though it's nowhere in my family history. The doctor dubbed me a 'spontaneous mutation.'

To say my outlook was bleak is an understatement. Certain doctors advised my parents to expect nothing from my short life, others said I should be institutionalized, and I'm pleased to say my parents ignored them all.

Osteogenesis Imperfecta has degrees of severity. Babies with Type II, in my era, tended to die soon after birth. In the 1950s and '60s, Type III babies, with their severe physical deformities, might reach age 10. Someone with Type IV, my condition, could expect a 'slightly shortened' lifespan, and while the physician who predicted my early death is long dead, I'm alive and thriving with a story to inspire others in their own stories.

As I write, I'm 66 years old, 4'2" tall, and in a wheelchair. In my college (yes, college) days, I was an elite wheelchair athlete. I competed in basketball and track. At one point I ranked third in the world in the one-mile run. For 43 years I've owned and ran health and fitness clubs.

A 4'2" guy in a wheelchair owning gyms. Crazy, huh? I've coached teams, overseen hundreds of employees, married, and divorced. Yes, married, though unkind kids in my school years said it would never happen.

PEOPLE DON'T FAIL, THEY GIVE UP

Imagine you're on a nice walk through a quiet street when a huge man—6'6", say, with bulging biceps and triceps—appears and punches you in the gut. You crumble to the ground, eyes watering with pain, writhing until you can catch your breath. When you manage at last to pick yourself up, and he punches you again.

The two-million-dollar question is: How many gut punches before you stay down? Or who tires first—you or him? How many times do you get back up, and who will tire first? Because the attacker is LIFE, and every one of us arrives on this planet in circumstances perfectly tailored to disrupt the nice walk we think we deserve. How we navigate, or succumb to our disruptions, is how we write our story.

We can't control our attacker, but we're no less in charge of our stories because we control the outcome—of this I'm certain—when we get back up. What I've discovered throughout my life as an athlete, a coach, a husband, and a businessman is that when people say they 'failed' at something, upon deeper inspection they simply threw in the towel. Giving up in adversity is increasingly common with each passing day. The number of young people committing suicide or falling to drug and alcohol abuse, the people failing at marriage, all beg the question: Is life so unbearably difficult, or do people just give up too easily?

GOODNESS WHILE SUFFERING

By the time I was 12 years old, I'd had more than 80 broken bones. Most of my childhood I spent in traction or a body cast, chest to toes, not from playing football, or skiing, or drag racing, but from a sneeze, a cough…maybe I turned too quickly and hit something.

After a while a person becomes an expert on his attacker. Even as a kid, I could name my broken bone sooner than the doctor could. Or I'd name it for my parents to tell the doctors and speed my getting the right treatment.

I was both an accident waiting to happen and a boy whose spirit craved adventure. One day when I was nine years old and watching kids in the neighborhood, my dad went into the garage and built me a car mechanic's dolly. Lying belly down in my full body cast, I could propel it with my hands, flying low to the ground into a big, wide world of possibilities.

And with that first burst of dolly-borne freedom, my faith soared. In the suffering and limitations, God was handing me adventure. Hope coursed through my veins and looped around my fragile bones. On a magic carpet of wood and wheels, I was invincible, certain that my physical challenges would paradoxically unlock my future, certain that somewhere inside I was whole and unbroken.

Unlimited belief packs its own power, and a day came when I graduated from the dolly to a wheelchair. In my teens, as I fractured less frequently, I took on and excelled in sports.

WHAT IS HOPE?

To hope is to confidently expect positive outcomes.

In my roles as athlete, business owner, keynote speaker, and writer I meet thousands of people more shattered of soul than I am in my body. Of the two, it's also true that broken hope is far more crippling. My hope has been bruised but unbroken, and for that I credit the unshakable, unbreakable truth that God has good for me. I repeat: Despite the pain and the setbacks—past, present, and future—all that God has for me is good. Since the first day I've known that hope deep in my broken bones, I've wanted to share it with broken souls.

Hope is nothing a person can see or touch or taste. Try to slice it with a sword, punch away at it, but to no avail. And yet it emanates from anyone who has it, sparkling with optimism, impervious to attack.

You and you only may choose hope. You alone choose whether to believe that good is ahead or that "the other shoe is about to drop." No matter the circumstances, every person has the power and authority to live a life of victory, or a life laced with defeat, to go on or to give up, to quit or to take the next step. *Hope—the belief in ever-present good—can lift and carry us through the worst times and set us down in victory, but the choice is ours alone.*

DEFEAT OR VICTORY IS ALWAYS WITHIN YOUR GRASP

I chose victory, and with God's help I've held to that choice. My life has no outside fixes, but with every fiber of my being I know that my life is not only good but amazing. The secret, which I love to share, is that when I *believe* my life is good, when I have absolute faith in that truth, when I expect good, I attract good.

WHEN I LOOK FOR THE GOOD IN EVERYTHING AND EVERYONE... *I EXPERIENCE GOOD!*

Think of it this way. Regardless of my circumstances, pain or discomfort, when my hands are outstretched, palms facing down, God's blessings fall to the ground around me, ungrasped and unrecognized. Conversely, when I stretch out my hands, palms up, when I expect good to fall into them, I receive what a Good God longs to give me.

"Character cannot be developed in ease and quiet," said Helen Keller, the Michael Jordan of turning adversity into hope. "Only through experience of trial and suffering can the soul be strengthened." She also warned that security is mostly a superstition, and that "life is a daring adventure or nothing."

True, the 'blessing' of my apparently devastating physical 'handicap' may have given me a stronger impetus to find courage, yet whatever happens to us is ours to embrace as something God can use to inspire others.

The last time I broke a bone I was 41 years old, headed to a concert in my sport wheelchair. At the time I was a part-time pastor, full-time business owner, living alone and unmarried. Brittle bone disease makes a person hyper-vigilant. For instance, I've never consumed alcoholic beverages to the point of becoming drunk. A clear head and awareness of my surroundings is integral to my wellbeing. The evening of the concert, in my excitement I overlooked the irregular concrete leading into the venue. My wheelchair flipped, landing me eight feet away, aware instantly that my left femur and scapula were broken, and that I'd be in a body cast for months.

What I couldn't know was how I'd manage or where I'd find help. My faith wavered, but God was ahead of me, arranging my next year. I held to my believe that God would protect my business and I would recover without having to spend months in a nursing home.

What happened? A woman from the church I pastored was a nurse, and she and her husband set up a hospital bed in their home. We held leadership meetings in my room. I counseled individual church members from my bed. I even taught Sunday school in my room, flat on my back in a chest-to-toes body cast. One evening one of my caregiver-hosts overheard a counselee say to me, "You don't understand how tough it is."

From my hospital bed, in a full body cast, I couldn't identify with *difficulty*. Hope, or the lack of it, can cause that sort of misimpression. Though I was the one laid out and broken, the man with me saw no suffering. *He* was the one suffering.

THE HEALING POWER OF UNBREAKABLE HOPE

The challenges in our lives that feel custom-designed to break us are the ones God uses to lead us to our best selves. Living with broken-bone disease I became a world-class athlete. From a wheelchair I built standup businesses. With the challenges of marriage and divorce I was always one sneeze, one cough, one unseen obstacle away from another potential break...and consequently I grew.

As a result, for a long time I've had no problems, only opportunities to strengthen my faith in an ever-present good God. Unbreakable hope is the straightest path to peace and prosperity. When you have it, all you see is the good that spreads before you as you catch your breath and get up, again and again, from the latest punch. When you have it, every new blow is a chance to see what new wonder awaits. When you have it, instead of giving into darkness, your light helps others find the same indestructible adventure.

Wherever you are in your life, my prayer is that no matter the challenge you face, my story can help you exercise your hope like a muscle, growing stronger by the day as you continue to write your story.

The man on the street may seem to have your number. The punches will come, and you will fall, but you can also get back up. You have more in your tank than you think. From an auto-mechanic's dolly to championship athletics, from divorce to the ups and downs of building businesses, I can tell you not to fear what hits you.

…The adventure is in getting back up!

About Gary

Don't be deceived by the easy smile, Gary Patti knows more than a little about knockdowns and rebounds. These days as a keynote speaker, life coach, business consultant, and bestselling author, his unique comeback story is teaching others how to stay in the game and win.

Gary was a two-week-old infant when a fractured femur (thigh bone) led to a diagnosis of Osteogenesis Imperfecta—brittle-bone disease. Before he was 12, he would have 80 fractures; as an adult he'd land in a body cast for months at a time. Instead of a sheltered existence, however, Gary's remarkable life and career came together while mending through 100 broken bones and a dozen-plus surgeries.

In his late teens, the man up for a challenge played wheelchair basketball for the University of Illinois. Post college, he competed at home in New Jersey. Then came his real game: long-distance road races, starting with runs in which he was the only one not on foot. Before companies were building wheelchairs to race, Gary had designed and built his own. By 1977, in the wheelchair mile, he ranked third in the world. Then in 1979 in New Jersey, he opened a 2,500-square foot health club that expanded to a 20,000 sq ft facility. Soon after he became managing-partner of a five-health-club chain.

Calling it 'unbreakable hope,' Gary has fielded business pressures, bankruptcy, and marriage betrayal. In 2009, he faced down prostate cancer, bringing his unconventional optimism to more kinds of physical healing. To people in businesses, the labor force, marriage, corporate America, school—young and old—his message now is to master the mindset that gives life: the belief that God has blessings and good plans for you. In 95 percent of the cases people don't fail, he says, they simply give up.

In 2023, Gary coauthored the bestselling book *Never Give Up* with hall-of-famer Dick Vitale. On the strength of his story there, his privilege now, he says, is to lift lives everywhere. He is an ordained pastor based in Southwest Florida; he's been a missionary to both South America and Asia.

What's Gary's whole story? What makes a 'broken' man a hero to so many?

Learn more at:
- garypatti.com
- unbreakablehope.com
- Tel: 908-377-3751

CHAPTER 10

WOUNDED HEALER

BY JENNIFER PERRI

I'm not a victim. That's the risk I take in telling you this. But there are women who know—the hard way—what I've been through. And my business, literally, is helping turn backstories like theirs into comeback stories like mine.

In high school I was a top student – popular and invincible. I bypassed college to be a wife and mother: what I was supposed to want, I thought. In high school home economics in those years, junior and senior girls like me absorbed adult life along a preset route. What no class or degree could prepare me for was a decade of terror when the person who vowed to love, honor, and defend me became my abuser, stripping my control, threatening my family, churning my life into a whitewater forking at last into prison and divorce. I have three beautiful boys, no regrets there. But when the rapids hit, my raft swirled and bobbed with no navigation, nothing to grab.

Abuse isolates like an invisible wall, deflecting friends and family members, making them unsure how to help, blocking the victims' impulses to reach out. "How stupid to stay," some people will say, but they say it out of ignorance. No one on the outside can know the world inside. A bullied woman's hesitations weave through shame, religion, finances, fears for the children…

Had it not been for the severity, I might never have left. The final blowup ended with my first husband in prison and my final exit, though getting out is one thing and knowing where to go is another. Ninety-nine percent of escapees have no plan, no map, no landmarks, no paved road back to normal life. Like most abused women, I'd be finding my own way.

And like most abused women, I'd be starting over at a deficit. While my friends went to college, found first jobs, and started families and careers, I was a new mom in chaos. So it was that I entered the workforce for the first time in my late twenties, to pay my bills, yes, but to make good my promise to myself to be the professional I'd searched for and couldn't find—the woman who understood my life and what I'd needed.

From the valley of my own ignorance, I went into financial services, eventually joining a firm, determined to help other women coming out of their traumas. Every life change has one; financial firms know that. What I knew were the hard traumas: the brutality, mental wounds, physical violence, isolation, divorce, single-parenting, and remarriage. Besides financial help, I left my trauma needing a GPS to locate my surroundings and myself. And so began an extremely successful financial advisory niche.

Even now it's hard to volunteer that I've been married several times, but it's part of my story. After the marriage that rewrote my life, within a short period I remarried a man who was nice to me, a mistake quickly obvious to us both. And if a divorce can be ideal, ours was.

A diagnosis of PTSD explains much of this time—the years I was out but not free: in a fog, needing to heal, needing a place to land, and missing the tarmac. The short version, to use a different metaphor, is that just when I thought I was out, the hole deepened and widened around me. I'd fought my years of damage by fighting for others but that didn't heal my wounds—

in part because no one understood them. No one had walked in my shoes or on my road.

"I can't comprehend…I can't imagine what you've been through," counselors would say. Of course they couldn't. It took me 28 years to start to address not my children, not other women, not a career, not a new husband, but myself. When I finally did, it helped to have an ally in the form of my husband of the last five years, my soulmate, the profound presence in my life—a love story for another time. The professional who came alongside me was an expert in PTSD, someone able to say, "Me, too," even if not to the same degree.

For too many years the words "How does that make you feel?" had felt anemic. I needed someone to feel what I felt, to know the wanting to give up, to take our own lives, to forever shut out any new chance to love. That person in my life lit my path to a new sense of worth.

And here's what happened: When I started to love myself, to affirm myself daily, to create vision boards of what I wanted, to begin to rebuild, like great land masses joining in my psyche, the big pieces came together.

"And the end of all our exploring will be to arrive where we started and know the place for the first time," the poet T.S. Eliot wrote. Coming back to my mended self, I knew I would spend the rest of my life helping other women. All of that came together for me on Dec. 20, 2021, the day I woke up in my bed feeling strange. By the end of that day I was on my back in the hospital, paralyzed, diagnosed with Guillain-Barre.

It was that quick. One day is a normal routine, the next I'm in a hospital bed, arms, and legs frozen, still sharing my optimism with doctors and nurses as they brushed in and out of my room. Would I walk again, I'd ask, and the silence screamed because no one could know. Even now, people with cases less severe than mine are still in wheelchairs. Guillain-Barre is a mystery with data points instead of treatments. My first steps were more than a year away, I was told. But I took my first steps 56 days out of hospital, and I continue to bust every milestone

My deficit days are behind me. Especially now. I'll not be asking, "What is this doing to me?" but "What will I do with this?" Even from a wheelchair, problems can only broaden my path. Besides financial issues, abuse, divorce, and single parenting, my massive medical episode opened my eyes and heart to more hurting people.

Why was I assigned another mountain? I don't know, but I can show other people that mountains can move. Whatever blocks our path, it's in us to alter the topography—from within ourselves or with someone's help. I wouldn't be here if it weren't so.

In my weeks in the hospital, the flowers, cards, texts, and visits came from people I'd once inspired with my words. Now they inspired me, some of them re-sending the very words I'd sent them. Beautiful. For the most resilient people, low times will come. Some days others carried optimism for me until I had it again for myself.

Today I am a transformational coach specializing in divorce, empowerment, money, and mindset. I help my beloved clients create the lives they want with affirmations, vision boards, moving from a scarcity mindset to an abundant one, removing mental mountains.

I believe in better endings because I'm writing my own. I live in the mountains and in the house that one day existed only on my vision board. Every item on every board, in fact, has come down as I affirm and activate it. I'm a best-selling author and a producer because life brings opportunities, and when an opportunity aligns with what I do and it can help change lives, I'm in.

The aftereffects of Guillain-Barre can last for years. Some days I still wake up unable to walk well. Some days the last thing I want to do is get up out of bed, read my affirmations or project anything positive. But I clear my head enough to do it because words have power, ideas have power, and affirmations make a difference.

I'm not a victim—that's the risk in telling this story. But there are women who know, the hard way, what I've been through, and I tell it for them. Because my business now—make that my life—is helping turn backstories like theirs into comeback stories like mine.

About Jennifer

Jennifer Perri is a Transformational Life Coach, Certified Divorce & Empowerment Coach and 2x Best-Selling Author and she has spent over two decades helping women transform their lives. Jennifer's mission is to empower women to live financially fearless, embrace their inner worth and become the sheroes in their stories.

Jennifer stands as a living testament to the indomitable human spirit. With a beautiful life, a loving husband, and a fulfilling career, she has triumphed over adversity and emerged stronger than ever. Jennifer's journey, though marred by hardship, has equipped her with the unwavering resolve to effect change in the world. With each client she empowers, each life she touches, she continues to rewrite the narratives of resilience and triumph, proving that we all have the power to craft our own destinies.

Jennifer has been featured in the media as a thought leader, appearing on or in ABC, NBC, FOX, CBS, *Vanity Fair* (February 2022, Atlanta Woman Feature), *The Tycoon Magazine, Newsweek, Fortune*, and *Forbes*. She has been a contributor to two international best-selling books, *Dare to Succeed* with Jack Canfield, creator of the *Chicken Soup for the Soul* series and her most recent book, *Quiet and Badass.*

For more information or to connect with Jennifer, visit:

- www.jenniferperri.com

CHAPTER 11

KEEP MOVING FORWARD: #KMF

BY GUY COLANGELO

It was three words—an aside from a boss early in my career. He was reviewing a snafu, talking about next steps. Buried in one of his comments, all he said was, "Keep moving forward."

You won't see that line etched into a memorial, but the it's the spirit of every memorial you'll ever see. My boss went on talking that day, but I had the relief a person feels when he finally gets the words to the tune in his head.

'Keep moving forward' became my life motto.

It was still just a tune when I was sixteen years old and took over a friend's business driving college students home on holidays. You could say I didn't know much then, but looking back, I see top-level instincts. Freshmen and sophomores at the college had to live on campus without cars. In the fall their parents dropped them off, but for breaks the drives got inconvenient.

The first thing I did was reidentify the customer. My friend had tacked his flyers on dorm bulletin boards, appealing to students with tight budgets and low standards. But wasn't it their parents who were driving the cars and writing checks? I got the families' home addresses and sent them letters about my story and service. At parent-student events, I showed up to put a face with a promise.

My friend had contracted with bargain drivers and buses. I secured top companies with high safety records and tripled the travel fees. To me it was all common sense. To my booming list of clients it was relief. Stacks of envelopes with checks crowded into the Colangelo family mailbox. I was still 16 years old and heading to the bank to open my first business account.

For two years of high school and most of college, 'moving forward' kept me on the move. Then in my senior year, the original owner reclaimed the business, and just like that, I was back on my own. Yep, it stung. I'd been flying; now I felt dropped over a cliff.

I can't tell you what was going through my mind in those hard months, or why I didn't throw in the towel. I'm pretty sure it was that tune in my head. Then, when I signed up for the intro to marketing course in college, the business already under my belt put me miles ahead of my peers. The day of the first lecture on direct marketing, I beelined to my prof's office to talk about marketing careers. After that I took every marketing course in my degree. Data mining (now 'big data') hooked me with its hard numbers and measurable results. Before I ever put on a cap and gown, I was the marketing manager in a regional company.

One day my first boss confided to me that the candidates for my position had come down to me and a young woman with an MBA. When I asked him why he chose me, he said, "Because of your story and your entrepreneurial spirit." That revelation gave me the confidence to keep doing what I know how to do. It also showed me the limits of an MBA. I'm glad I held onto the job instead of sidelining for a statistics program in big data.

Is it just me, or do mentors await us around every corner? In my second job, I grew under the influence of Richard Cross, a big-time direct marketer for the Consumers Union, the non-profit publisher of Consumer Reports. Before the Internet, Consumer Reports was ground zero for product research. In the 1980s, it was only months from closing its doors when Richard stepped in to insert a fund-raising campaign in the annual-report surveys. In my life, Richard stands tall for teaching me not just marketing tactics but marketing principles, not just the what but the why. He made me fluid to any marketing challenge, any industry trend, in any era.

What he taught me became the heartbeat of my message...

Change is inevitable; keep moving forward.

In that spirit, I learned that doors open and doors close. I learned to focus not on a room I can't enter, but on where I ultimately want to be. I learned determination, the opposite of giving up. By way of a small example, as a Florida resident, when a hurricane cancels my flight to a big game out of town, I stay on the airline sites for changes and updates. I study driving options. Until I'm sure I *have* to stay anywhere, I stay informed.

Maybe as you began reading this piece you glanced at my Italian surname. I belong to a people group—and to a big group of people—who love to eat. One byproduct of those enthusiastic family get-togethers can be extra weight, and recently I said goodbye to 120 pounds that needed to go. It wasn't a matter of a change here and there. It was lifestyle overhaul. Going in I knew I'd have to hit reset on every daily routine. When people ask me how I pulled that trigger, I compare it to any addict who hits rock bottom. A day comes, I say, when you have to do something different, period.

"But how did you stay with it?" someone will ask. "A hundred and twenty pounds don't disappear with a strong wish." The hardest pounds were the last twenty, that's for sure. But I never considered quitting. By now the tune in my head played like a march, I knew I would keep moving forward.

That said, not all motivation is internal. From the beginning, certain people and events worked on me like power drinks. In the very first week, I lost thirteen pounds, my snoring disappeared, and I slept better. There's inspiration. With healthier fuel in me, I gained new energy. You'll think I'm making this up, but I also got more smiles from strangers in the checkout lines. It's true. And I was the one smiling when I could tighten the seatbelt strap on the airplane, leaving another 12 inches unused. It's another mental pickup to have access to better clothes.

As for roadblocks, the surprise was that they came most often from people close to me, as my new food choices disrupted old extended-family patterns. On the other hand, as my wife and I changed our food and health habits, our kids changed theirs. My oldest son got a trainer and got in shape. As I keep moving forward, my household moves forward too.

No one lives unto himself. I can't say that often enough. People watch and learn from what we do, and there's always more to learn and know from the people around us. We listen and observe, we learn, we filter what we learn through our own judgment. We tend to lock onto the lessons from people we admire. In college, it was my marketing professor. In my first job, my boss modeled how to treat people and handle situations. Then came Richard Cross, a graduate-level education in himself. As some wise person has put it: When the student is ready, the teacher will come.

What I've learned is that most development, professional or personal, turns on three things: 'want to, 'chance to,' and 'how to.'

(1) 'Want to' is the desire to change.
(2) 'Chance to' is the opportunity to act on that desire.
(3) 'How to' refers to a person's knowledge and ability.

KEEP MOVING FORWARD: #KMF

My son recently earned a place on a travel baseball team. When I say he earned it, he earned it. The first season after COVID, when we drove him to evaluations, he couldn't hit a ball, or catch one, or throw one to save his life. He cried all the way home. He said, "I suck at baseball!"

I said to him, "It's not about what just happened but what you do going forward. There are ways to not suck at baseball, and as long as you want to play, I'll support you." No question my son loves the game. His disappointment was obvious, but so was his *want to*.

As the dad, I made it my business to help with the *chance to* and *how to*. Recreation leagues are run mostly by dads like me, limiting opportunities for poor players to learn and advance. We got my son into baseball lessons. We enrolled him in an academy, where an ex-MLB pro gave him valuable tips. I watched him come through with the *want to*, and his hard work paid off. He got onto a real team by hitting, throwing, and catching well. People tend to give up too easily. I got to watch my son keep moving forward.

In my own school years I excelled at baseball. Once I hit a home run, and as I was going down the first baseline, I heard the opposing coach say to an assistant coach, "That kid is going somewhere." In ninth grade, meanwhile, every chance we got, my friends and I were playing roller hockey in the streets. That first year of high school I traded my concentration on baseball to include roller hockey, and I still regret it. Our hockey team won the league championship, but time away from baseball made me increasingly less viable to the other players, and I never regained the momentum. In tenth grade, I had the skills, but I didn't make the team.

I'd wanted a break from baseball. I'd felt plateaued. But those are insufficient reasons to quit. I wish my parents had urged me that time to keep moving forward. My life might be no different today for it, but I'd have no regret for not seeing a talent through. That poor choice to move sideways, I think, had a lot to do with my resolve now to always be moving forward.

No one decision can dictate a person's future. I tell my children that because I believe it. We can make excuses, or we can make good time. If I could bless my kids with one attitude, it would be the one that played in my head until I finally found the words in an authority figure who cared about me.

> *Until you die, I tell them, nothing is ever over.*
> *Keep moving forward.*

About Guy

Say hello to Guy Colangelo, a dynamic force in the realm of direct response marketing. For over two decades, he's been architecting and driving powerful campaigns that really ramp up sales. His journey started when he was just 16, with his first sales letter that had people enthusiastically sending back checks!

After a thrilling academic journey at the University of Central Florida, Guy jumped into the vibrant world of independently-owned boutique hotels. He conceptualized and led groundbreaking direct response campaigns with some of the largest airline loyalty programs in the world.

Then came his role as a Marketing Director for a subscription-based construction project information service provider. There, he built a powerhouse marketing department from the ground up that excelled in digital marketing, SEO, content marketing, email marketing, and so much more. His exemplary efforts earned him the tag "Lead Nirvana" from a renowned marketing technology firm.

Following this, Guy played a pivotal role at an automotive direct response agency as their Director of Marketing. He took member acquisition to new heights, driving the company to record-breaking revenues.

Today, Guy is at the helm of one of the largest personal branding agencies, running the day-to-day operations as their Chief Operating Officer. His strategic guidance and operational expertise continue to propel the company towards new levels of success.

Throughout his career, Guy's approach has been enriched by wisdom imparted by some of the great minds in direct marketing. This unique blend of time-tested marketing principles with today's fast-paced digital environment is his secret sauce to success.

Away from the corporate world, Guy, a native of Long Island, now basks in the sunshine of Orlando, FL with his wife, their two energetic sons, and their lovable Bernedoodle named Marty McFly. When he's not steering his team towards groundbreaking marketing strategies, he's either showing off his culinary chops in the kitchen or planning his next big overseas adventure.

And that's Guy - a dedicated marketer with a passion for his craft, a seasoned leader driving operational excellence, and a bon vivant with an infectious zest for life!

CHAPTER 12

REAL ESTATE IN AN UNREAL YEAR

BY AMBER NOBLE

True strength is not about proving how invincible you are, but rather being strong for others in their time of need.
~ Laila Ali

My client was a gentleman—well-traveled, a serial entrepreneur, ready now to slow down. His mother had adopted him, and we were selling his childhood home, in the family for generations. Now the plot takes a sharp turn because the house was paid in full, that he was sure of, but no satisfaction letter existed to prove it. The mortgage company was long closed...and oh, yes, there were multiple wills with varied versions of his mother's final wishes.

Any other year my client would have gone to his mother's bank, worked through the chain of command, and gotten his hands on the right papers. But this was the spring of 2020, when all the COVID-19 news 'over there' in China or Italy suddenly affected every person and business I knew.

Remember the mental whiplash? One night we go to bed busy

with life and lives and properties. The next morning we live in a country frozen in fear. The professional world of real estate is about big plans, big costs, big decisions, big moves. My clients were calling me in 'big' despair. Families that were packed to relocate to new states and even new continents were watching sales implode and careers plummet.

There are services that will track down long-buried paperwork and dissolve legal knots, but in the world of pandemics and panic, my client and I fell into a rabbit hole of automated messages and dead ends. With every rejection of a potential buyer, his house's marketability and price-tag dropped.

Hear the pain? My business card says real estate, but my work is advocacy and high-level problem solving. I help people and families use ownership to build multi-generational wealth and create legacy. In the case of the missing 'sat' letter, my client's ownership was everything to his legacy and his future. What wouldn't I do to help him? From contractor names to pre-inspection punch lists, as the world locked up in mid-stride, I helped him get the workers he needed in and out of his home. I guided him through real estate laws and technology, tapping resources and building rapport with other agents whose buyers were cooled on the idea of a home purchase. We made it work but it wasn't easy, and the stress showed in my reacquaintance with insomnia.

"Don't give up," I'd say to him. "Just a little longer. We got this!" Two or three times a week, he and I would mask up and meet in his mother's living room. "Here's everything we're doing," I'd say, pulling out my written game plan. "We're gonna be all right."

And then it happened. On a typical 2020 day when headlines were grim and neighborhood parks were crowded with restless people sheltering in place, the satisfaction papers showed up. Not long after that the will settled, and the closing took place in a parking lot. And there we all were: me (on behalf of my client), the title company rep, the buyer, and their agent, all masked and gloved, signing papers in shifts on the tailgate of a truck.

That was my professional world. Privately I was dissolving my nearly 15-year marriage, selling that home, and settling into a new home with my daughter. Upending my life was one thing, but Leah needed consistency, especially at school, and not just any school. So, as America hunkered down and companies shuttered, as employees and even lovers learned to work and relate by Zoom, I went to great lengths to help my clients sustain their lives. Off the radar my daughter and I were doing our best to carve out a new life. To the side, as a landlord of 20-plus years I carried multiple mortgages on my own portfolio of properties, housing several tenants no longer paying rent.

Grit is generational, at least mine is. In the pre-Civil Rights Era, my mom grew up in the roughest section of North Philadelphia, which is saying something. She was a nurse, a nurturer, a former teen mom who pulled herself up and out of brutal circumstances. My dad was an Army veteran and a welder for 30 years for the Philly school board until a career-ending back injury on the job. But that's not half of what he did. On the side he owned and self-managed multi-family duplex apartments, single-family houses, and a bar and lounge, doing much of the superintendent and maintenance work himself. As a little girl on excursions with Dad to collect rent and make repairs, the real estate bug bit me early.

By the time my father succumbed to COPD in 2007, he was an amputee, a fighter to the end. Mom is a stroke survivor, the other source of my work ethic—my mama-bear mentality, my servant-leader mindset, my will to figure it out and get it done against all odds. Find a way or create a way, they taught me, but never give up.

With the best of my parents coursing through my veins and fiduciary responsibilities for 25 to 50 sets of lives, in 2020 I waded into government restrictions, Zoom protocol, virtual school requirements, and changing homes with…well, to be precise, with sweat, hutzpah, journaling, and prayer. Almost daily, for each client—and for Leah and me—I updated my book of gameplans: these goals, these steps, these people, this information, this action, these resources.

Across America, 2020 became a graduate-level course in change and adaptation. For me it was a review course in my values and perceptions—reminding me to take nothing for granted, not even getting up and going to work, or walking the aisles of a grocery store, or seeing a doctor when I'm sick or my child had a stubborn cough. I've never lived paycheck to paycheck, but I saw colleagues forced to give up. I saw 2020 clean house in real estate, dropping professionals there for the wrong reasons, or the ones who took their real estate exams expecting a cakewalk.

Real estate is more than door keys, open houses, and clever social media. People come to specialists like me with big portions of their lives in the balance, needing us to care about their outcome as much as they do. And I do. And it's not just clients I'm responsible for, my colleagues depend on me in their livelihoods, as I do them.

Leah is thriving, by the way. I see so much of my mother in this little girl we once feared might never talk. Leah just turned eleven and is headed to the sixth grade. She is popular, dynamic, creative, talented—busting autism stereotypes right and left. Mom is meticulous, committed to the details; that's the nurse in her, alert to potential symptoms, double and triple checking. And that's one of Leah's autistic superpowers: details. People on the spectrum aren't expected to show empathy, but Leah is the most empathetic person I know—like Mom. Dad was resourceful. When he shut down his businesses he opened a driving school. Close a path, and he'll find a way. That's me and Leah, too.

Grit is in our DNA, yet it's still a choice. I always say my difference is what makes a difference, and everything different about me is why I'm here. At the end of my life, my regret would be to die or leave this earth without imparting all the best of what I have learned and of who I am to other people, starting with those closest to me.

It took a lifetime to prepare for all that 2020 brought—the year that often seemed like a lifetime. But by the end of it, what did I see? The best of my roots and all that I am.

HOW TO TAKE ON A STORM OF A YEAR—OR ANY YEAR—WITHOUT LOSING YOURSELF

1. Anchor in something or someone bigger than you.

In 2020, as always, my anchor was my faith in the omnipresent power of God, unceasing certainty that if I prayed, if I stayed present and persistent, not even a pandemic could stop me. Wherever you drop anchor, you want to find and retreat to quiet spaces to listen to your own breath, to hear yourself think. The art of meditation, centering yourself, and calming yourself to a point of understanding, benefits body, mind, and spirit.

2. Commit to health and wellness.

Our minds and bodies require nourishment to help other minds and bodies. If I rescue my clients from precarious home sales and purchases, while looking after my elderly parents, while caring for my precious daughter, while trying to save the world, but fail to prioritize my own well-being, I am sure to implode and hurt others in the fallout. Your flight attendant is right: Put on your own oxygen mask before assisting others.

3. Let a day be a day.

Give all you can give in the day you have, then shut it down to start again with a new day. My name is Amber Noble, and I am a workaholic in recovery. In 2007, when I transitioned from media and entertainment to real estate, I had one gear and it was high. What saved me was learning that a person can shut down at night, recharge, and reset to fight for her clients another day. In the world of real estate— considerably more "purpose driven" than my former industries—I have learned to mix my commitment with mindfulness.

About Amber

Amber Noble is known for many things; an unselfish contributor, thought-leader, highly skilled business strategist, masterful negotiator, people-connector, dynamic speaker, experienced Real Estate Wealth-Building Advisor and Investor/Landlord with over 20 years of expertise.

As an award-winning Realtor®, Amber helps clients build generational wealth and financial security each year in PA and NJ. She specializes in assisting first-time homebuyers and high net worth luxury home sales, ultimately helping nearly 500 individuals and families accumulate $200 million in real estate assets.

Additionally, Amber serves as the Managing Broker of Record overseeing New Jersey licensees within two Keller Williams Realty market centers that are responsible for producing billions in annual sales volume.

Before her successful real estate career, Amber enjoyed an accomplished career in marketing, brand strategy, and product management in the Radio, TV, and Music industries, with roles in major companies including Radio One, ABC Television and Def Jam Records.

For more than half a decade, Amber played a pivotal role on advising, marketing, and quarterbacking album rollouts for globally recognized recording artists including Jay-Z, LL Cool J, Patti LaBelle, Lionel Richie, The Roots, Eve and 112 to name a few.

For over a decade, Amber, the Founder & CEO of I For Talent Consulting & Advisory (formerly I For Talent Management), has represented her partner in business and friend, Laila Ali, a retired, hall of fame boxing world-champion and daughter of the late Muhammad Ali.

Amber also devoted nearly two decades developing, guiding and day-to-day overseeing the career of a familiar former radio host and HGTV personality. Amber went on to later manage the celebrity DJ'ing and budding music career of popular actor, Idris Elba during his days as Stringer Bell on HBO's cult-classic series, *The Wire*.

Amber is a successful writer who significantly contributed to the Amazon real estate book, *Keep Calm...It's Just Real Estate: Your No-Stress Guide To Buying A Home*. She has published other best-selling books she previous co-authored including, *Mastering The Art of Success* with Jack Canfield, known for *Chicken Soup For The Soul*. Her next upcoming title is *Empathy and Understanding in Business*, co-authored with other successful entrepreneurs and Chris Voss, the former Chief FBI Negotiator and *The New York Times* Best Selling Author of *Never Split The Difference*.

Amber's advocacy work extends to seniors, individuals on the Autism spectrum, and special needs parents, driven by her personal experiences. She established the Noble Acts Of Kindness Foundation to support those in need. Amber takes pride in being a dedicated mother to her amazing 11-year-old daughter, Leah.

Amber holds a Bachelor's degree from Temple University, she earned an advanced certificate from Harvard Law School's Negotiation program, is a Certified Negotiation Expert®, Certified Luxury Home Marketing Specialist®, and possesses various specialized real estate designations.

Connect with her at: AmberNoble.com

CHAPTER 13

THE GAME OF POSSIBILITY: SA-ME-ZA

BY BABLY BHASIN

The noise reached my ears as I was putting the children to bed—guttural sounds, animal-like. I tucked in my girls and hurried to the surreal sight of my husband convulsed in deep, agonizing howls. The date was June 14, 2015, three days after his 41st birthday.

"Bably, I love life! I want to live!" he said feverishly, seeing me in the doorway of our bedroom. "I don't understand why this is happening."

No one understood. The world-renowned oncologist Dr. Ang Peng Tiam was as shocked as we were when I broke the news to him over the phone. For the past six months, he had gone to extremes to cure my husband's father of lymphoma. Now, unrelated to his father's diagnosis, a biopsy of the bumps on Pankaj's head reported Acute Lymphoblastic Leukemia (ALL).

In our bedroom that night, Pankaj and I held each other, trying not to cry. "We just beat cancer," I said. "We will do it again." Slowly, as calm and courage returned, so did Pankaj's appetite.

"Could you make something gourmet for me?" he said.

"How can you think about food, at this moment, Pankaj?" I said, wide-eyed.

Nobody loved and relished good food like my husband. He would exclaim in joy savoring every bite; the efforts of the cook couldn't be more valued. A few minutes later I set a beautiful tray before him.

He studied the plate and then looked at me. "When days are good and you come home to a good meal, you feel like a king," he said. "When days are bad and you come back to a good meal, it gives you hope. Feed me hope, Bably."

The next morning, a Monday, we met with Dr. Ang. The cancer was aggressive and he had to prescribe treatments to match. "It'll hit you like a nuclear bomb," he said.

"I hear possibility, Doc," Pankaj said with a great big smile. "Let's do this."

In that moment, standing in the doctor's office, I experienced a life-defining truth. In life, you can either play the game of probability or the game of possibility. Probability—whatever its number—means 'maybe.' Probability keeps you caged in self-doubt, self-distrust, and insecurity. Possibility, in contrast, is an unwavering belief. It gives you freedom from fear. It says, "I know who I am. I know where I want to go. I know why I want to get there. And that's all I need to know. Period."

Possibility is soul power.

As for me, my thoughts were also laced with anger. *How?* I'd think. *How?* Diabetes, heart disease, stroke—those I get. What the heck is this from nowhere?

Regardless, I too had to 'Pick a P.' As Mike Tyson famously said, "Everyone has a plan, until they get hit." I chose possibility, soulfully joining Pankaj in this wild, scary, unimaginable nuclear fallout. Time after time I would watch him take a hit and come back from the brink, only to take another.

In the harshest of times, the hardest-won essential is HOPE (*SANA means hope*). It's the possibility that 'the possible' is possible, that there is a light at the end of the tunnel. People will say hope is not a strategy, but I disagree. A strategy of hope inspires creativity and bold actions. It allows us to break the status quo, outside and within, and be open-minded to solutions beyond logic—to explore and become more than we think we can be.

With hope, even in the clouds of torture, I saw the power of the human body to survive extremes. Where others might roll into a ditch and give in, Pankaj never gave up. His motto, *"Whatever you do, always do it with character and integrity,"* kept him in the race. Integrity isn't just about what you do unto others, but also what you do unto yourself.

It was also a time of experimenting with new ingredients. My friend suggested papaya leaves to restore low platelet counts, as observed in dengue patients. Nights about 11 o'clock, when the neighborhood was quiet, I'd put my baby in the stroller, attach my other two daughters to my left and right and take to the sidewalks. Singing *I Believe I Can Fly*, we'd forage for young papaya leaves. Back at home, the girls would blend and extract the leaves' bitter, nasty liquid and serve it with a smile.

"Here Papa, drink the magic juice!" they'd say. Cancer tests the entire family.

In October 2015, Dr. Ang declared Pankaj cancer-free. Like a newborn, he couldn't wait to taste the goodies of life again. "I got my second chance!" he exclaimed, and with the second chance came peace.

But by October 2016, the cancer was back. Still determined, he continued his pre-cancer life schedule. He was a picture of love for life and human will. Watching him, Frank Sinatra's *My Way* would come to mind: "I faced it all, and I stood tall and did it my way."

Often his treatments and medicines spiked severe heat in his body. I'd bring bags of ice from the nearest 7-Eleven, fill the jacuzzi with freezing water, and watch him ease himself in, unblinking.

"Aren't you cold?" I'd ask, incredulous.

"If I think about it, I'll feel it," he'd say, settling into the frost as if it were a deck chair on a hot sunny day. "I'll cross the stream, I have a dream," he'd say, and then he'd sing *Stand By Me* with Ben E. King at the top of his lungs.

Slowly but surely we moved forward. Round two was working well. In December 2016, Pankaj was on his last leg of chemotherapy when test results of his marrow indicated a 0.0001 percent lingering cancer. Our hematologist, Dr. Lim Zi Yi, suggested a stem-cell transplant.

"Looks like possibility, I'm game," Pankaj said, unrelenting.

We were all home, reveling in the new year of 2017, when I heard Pankaj scream my name. Running into the bedroom I found him, shocked and shaking, scaring me more than anything so far. His face was cherry red and he could barely speak.

"Bubble," he said, "your father just passed away."

Silently, I went to the front door and walked out. "Don't come with me," I whispered. The night was black as coal, I looked up and said, "Dear God, I have two wings, my father and Pankaj. I've lost one wing today. Please don't take my other wing. My soul will shatter without him."

The next day I was on the plane to Delhi, downing drink after drink, in an effort to numb my thoughts and overwhelming feelings. "Enough is enough, dear God, I'm tired," were my last words before I fell asleep.

Besides attending the last rites of my father, I spent that week collecting saliva swabs, combing for stem-cell candidates among my husband's family members. What a picture: My father gone and me trying not to lose my husband.

"You're so calm," my sister-in-law said as I handed her a swab. "How the hell do you do it?"

I remember staring at the lines on my palm and saying, "If I give up, I'll be a dead man walking. And I…ain't dead yet. I see hope."

HOPE. DREAM. POSSIBILITY.

Pankaj's cousin Ashish, a 50 percent match, would be his donor. "The stem-cell transplant is barbaric," Dr. Lim warned us. "Pankaj's immunity will go to zero. His body must revive itself through this storm, and while it does, expect anything."

On August 1, 2017, a few days after the donor extraction, it was time to meet up with Dr. Lim. I climbed into the car and saw Pankaj walking toward me with confidence. In his hand was a rolled chart paper. Catching his eye, I cocked my head.

"You'll see it soon," he said getting in.

In the doctor's office, he was ready. "I always listen to you, Dr. Lim," he said smiling. "Today is my day." Moving to the conference table, he unrolled a detailed timeline of a standard lifespan, a horizontal line intersected with graphs and analyses. At the 40-year mark a visual axis separated the past and the future.

Here I encountered that the second and most-underrated essential is GRATITUDE for one's existence (***MEHR*** *means gratitude*). The man before us radiated respect for life. "I'm extremely lucky to have been chosen to live this life," Pankaj said softly. "Grateful for all the blessings and challenges that came my way, which let me express my mettle and realize my worth. Proud as a peacock, if I may say so, Doc. I never let the world define me."

On the chart, he placed his finger on the number 40. "Here I am," he said. Moving his finger to the right, he said, "Here is the rest of my life. I don't want to leave with unfinished dreams."

For a moment and a lifetime, we stood at the crossroads of Pankaj's hindsight, foresight, and nowsight: between years lived and the years he stood to lose. *"Dreams are soulful wishes,"* he'd say. *"When you make them happen, you honor your soul."*

"Heal me, Dr. Lim," he said. "Fight for me with all you've got, and I promise, I'll give you a fight to remember."

"No matter what happens, it's an honor to fight with you Pankaj," Dr. Lim said.

As you've rightly guessed by now, the third soul-igniting essential is SPIRIT (***NAWEZA*** *means "I can do it"*). It declares: "My mind has conceived it, and I believe I can achieve it." It inspires clarity and audacity. As General Maximus roared in the movie The Gladiator, "What we do in life, will echo in eternity."

Mid-August 2017, Pankaj went in for his stem-cell transplant. Brave as a lion, he shouted, "I'll be back!" A month later, pneumonia crept in and his body could fight no more. At age 43, my beloved left me with a timeline, with unfinished dreams, and with deep wisdom—a story for another book.

For 1,200 days – 30,000 hours – Pankaj and I fought the good fight, and the lessons were life-awakening. Four decades on this planet, and it took cancer to reveal the depths of life.

THE GAME OF POSSIBILITY: SA-ME-ZA

As we stood shoulder-to-shoulder with children, wives and husbands just like us, we saw that cancer doesn't discriminate within creed, color, background, status, or age. We were all in the same boat, fighting the same problems. We all feel the same pain, we all look for hope, and we all deserve better.

One particular visit to Dr Ang's office stands out in my mind. Pankaj and I were sitting on the sofa in the waiting room when Greta Thunberg appeared on TV in her famous speech. "What are you leaving behind?" she asked. Pankaj and I sat silent, each with our thoughts. Like a beaver gnawing on a tree, her question nibbled at our souls.

And then, in the chaos and unity of cancer, we found our answer and founded SAMEZA with the only health-transforming rice in the world. Named for our daughters—Sana, Mehr, and Naweza—it is our battle against cancer, against diabetes, against the status quo. Sameza was the regal superfood that had helped my husband fight his cancer, and it became a blessing for our fellow patients too. "OMG!" I exclaimed when we realized its power, "If this can heal cancer patients, when the body is in its most-critical state, imagine what it could do for everyone else!" Our black cloud finally revealed its silver lining.

Like Pankaj, and like you, I am on a timeline. I am grateful to be alive, audacious enough to dream big, and crazy enough to make the dreams happen. Once upon a time I thought legacy meant monetary freedom. Today, I know legacy is not what we leave for others, but what we leave *in* them. Let's leave a legacy that will make our children proud.

Why must you SA-ME-ZA too? Because you matter, your dreams matter, your life matters.

Here's to the mindful ones, the forward thinkers, the visionaries! Here's to the ones who don't want to live life just as it is…who want more…who provoke better! Here's to the bold, who dare to create a better reality...to the ones who choose to make it happen...to making decisions that lead forward—because these are the changemakers. And while some may see them as far out, I see legends – the ones who do give a damn.

About Bably

Bably Bhasin is the Founder and CEO of Sameza Pte Ltd, makers of the only health-transforming rice in the world. Launched in Singapore in 2016, Sameza is an award-winning, internationally acclaimed company that is gaining sweeping recognition worldwide for its Harvard Medical School accredited, health-transforming superfood, Sameza Vintage Collection (SVC).

This artisan superfood was designed exclusively for The Royal Families with elite requirements of luxurious quality, taste, nutrition and health; and is now available to the public. With prestigious awards like Great Taste and being named a 'Star Revelation' by Michelin Guide, Bhasin is making a global impact by revolutionizing the way people consume daily staples.

In 2015 Bably's husband was diagnosed with cancer. As she stood shoulder-to-shoulder with children, wives and husbands, facing this dreadful disease, she realized the power of her rice. SVC was the regal superfood that helped her husband fight his cancer and it became a blessing for their fellow patients too. "OMG! If this can heal cancer patients, when the body is in its most-critical state, imagine what it can do for everyone else."

In 2020, the company became the first contestant from Singapore to win The Virtual Shark Tank for its superfood. Sameza is named for her three daughters: SA is Sana, which means 'hope'. ME is Mehr, which means 'gratitude'. ZA is Naweza, which means 'I Can Do It'. SVC represents her battle against cancer, against diabetes, against the status quo. Why? Because we all deserve better…because every life matters.

In addition to being a 'Making-An-Impact' Entrepreneur, Bably is also an author, motivational speaker, poet, artist and designer. As a contributing author in *MindStirring Business Secrets*, an anthology presented by Kevin Harrington, Bably says, "The future belongs to those who will disrupt things today."

Bably Bhasin has been seen in *Michelin Guide, theAsianparent, Emperics Asia, The Wellness Insider, Food Navigator Asia, Clozette, Vanilla Luxury*, and has appeared on CNA938, MoneyFM89.3 and Ticker News radio affiliates across Asia. With an impactful start in Singapore, Sameza is now forging ahead into global markets to make this regal superfood accessible to millions worldwide.

Truly, Bably walks her life motto: "Whatever you do, always do it with character and integrity."

Get in touch at:
- Email: bably@sameza.com
- Website: www.sameza.com

CHAPTER 14

ECONOMICS IS LIFE

BY MARK WADE

In college I drove a beat-up old 1966 Chevy Biscayne. One day it came down with a flat in the middle of Main Street during rush hour in Madison, New Jersey, right in front of a tire shop. The owner saw my trouble and helped me push my car into his drive.

"You got a spare tire?" he said, and I had to tell him no.

"Where you headed?"

"Up the road to the college," I said. "I'm in school there."
He asked if I had any money, and when I shook my head, he turned and shouted, "Get him out of my driveway, and get him a used tire!"

The shop owner with the tolerance for clunkers and college kids was John Kerwin. In a few minutes my car rolled out with four used, working tires, and all he said was, "Come pay us when you can."

Later that week I was back at the shop with money and a box of doughnuts, and John and I chatted. As I was leaving he said, "What're you doing Sunday morning?"

NEVER GIVE UP

I said I'd be coming home from my bar cleaning job around 7 or 8 a.m.

"Stop by here," he said, "and I'll take you to a turkey shoot."

It wasn't what it sounds like. You shoot a shotgun at clay targets to win a turkey. I showed up and in truth the targets were little orange flying saucers, and I stunk at it. But John and I became friends and shooting buddies.

Several years later, when my career was underway, I stopped back by the shop for four new tires, and John and I rekindled our friendship. He said again, "What're you doing Sunday? Want to come to a turkey shoot?"

"Surely you remember that I stunk at that," I said, but this is a prime instance of my good fortune in making the world's best friends. John encouraged me, and I knew enough to stick with it. That's partly why the title of this book intrigued me. Never give up? Who knew a person could. I spent my formative years with the dial set at 'survival,' but looking back even survival was due to more than sheer pushing through. At critical times people like John showed up to help me steer the push.

In college I chose economics, or it chose me, under a professor who loved the subject and wanted me to love it too—another guide. Much later, during stage-four cancer and a triple bypass, people would appear to help guide my push then too.

I love people. My initial draw to trap shooting was the camaraderie, like in golf or bowling. You meet friends and compete, and then you all go out to dinner.

Yeah, okay, I was known to want to win. In 1992, I won the main event at The Grand American World Trap Shooting Championships, and I'll mention that win set two world records. First, it beat the largest field ever—4,562 shooters from 22 countries (larger shoots have formed since). Second, it won by two targets, and with the only perfect score of 100. Until then every win had been by one target or a tie. That's Greek to most folks, but it was the first such win ever, and the 'two targets' record still stands.

The point is that a pinnacle in my life began years before at a gun club with a man I met over a flat tire. On one of those Sundays with John, I was lamenting my poor performance when I saw an ad for a shooting coach in New Jersey, of all places. Kay Ohye had won multiple US clay target championships and taught shooting clinics all over the country. Just as impressive to my mind, he was less than 30 miles from me.

In our first lesson, I was shooting and hitting very little. He said to me, "When you point at the target, what do you see out there?"

"Which target? I see two targets," I said earnestly, and he started laughing. He said, "Close your left eye and try again." A target flew up, and I smoked it. He said, "Do it again." The next 10 or 12 in a row I hit pow, pow, pow. He said, "Your problem is cross-dominance vision." He became my coach and friend all the way to the world championship, and to this day.

My mother would say, "Mark, your friends are God's way of making up for your family." I agree that God has a way of allowing deficits so He can make them assets. I grew up in a rough part of Newark, New Jersey, in the 1960s and '70s when divorces were the exception, and my mom struggled to raise two boys on a waitress's income. Her remarriage to an auto mechanic added two more brothers. We had a roof over our head all the time and decent food on the table most of the time.

In those years, the doggedness in my mom showed up in me too, as in high school wrestling and judo, where at age 16 I won third in the state. One day in my junior or senior year, Mom let me know that any education for me past high school would likewise come down to tenacity. "I was in the diner today, and some of your friends' parents came in," she said. "They were talking about who's going to this college or that. Mark, if you want to go to college, you'll have to figure out how to get there."

I worked for a year to pay for my first semester, and then I matriculated. When people would ask me, "What then?" I'd tell them I'd figure it out. Through a string of semesters, besides working two or three jobs, I filed for every loan I could—whatever it took to get through—and I paid them all back eventually. A capital-T Truth is that I can do anything for a short period: do anything, endure anything – like simultaneous chemo and radiation cancer treatments when that time came.

When I started college, my cousin Anthony Cuppari was in pre-med, which struck me as intelligent, so I jumped on board too. After a year and a half, I had to take an elective, and I thought, "If I'm paying for this, I'm not taking some meaningless course," and I signed up for Economics 101.

A doctor ought to know more about money than I did, I figured. Neither of my parents had graduated from high school. They knew about labor, but not how to manage the low wages they earned for it. When I began hanging out at friends' homes I discovered that other families didn't argue constantly about money. They might argue, but not always about money, and certainly not the way my family did.

The economics elective that changed my life was under Dr. Bogan. Economics covers big concepts like scarcity, supply and demand, costs and benefits, and incentives. Economics is about choices. On a personal level, economics play out in our finances—in how we shepherd our bank accounts, earnings, investments, and more. In my study of resources, both global and personal, I learned the high value of information, judgment, experience, wisdom, responsibility…and critical decision-making.

This new world of wisdom about money was like discovering a vitamin deficiency I didn't know I had. I craved it on behalf of all the people in my life who needed it. I wanted a future of helping people avoid what my family had suffered in the extreme.

Goodbye health profession: Cousin Tony would be the surgeon. The cancer I knew was financial ignorance and I was after that. Professor Bogan was the chair of the department; I changed my major to economics, asked her to be my advisor, and I never turned back.

Through college, graduate studies, and certifications and courses and experience to master the corporate world and build my own companies, I learned a hundred ways to push and to value people. And in my wildest dreams I could not have imagined the return. From the streets of New Jersey, through the grace of God, and I mean that, to Southern California in a life I'd seen only on TV, I made the type of income I'd never dreamed of and met people and families I'd never imagined, whose lives I'd be privileged to help advance. When someone asks for my secret, the answer is I had no secret, no tricks. I just told myself I'd do the work no one else wanted to do. I'd hear, "We need someone to be in Tulsa on Sunday morning to talk to a group after church," and I'd raise my hand, thinking when an opportunity came along, maybe they'd remember the guy who always volunteered and got the job done. And those opportunities sure enough came up and so did my name.

I'm in my 44th year of the only work I've ever done, which speaks to my push and to my associates, clients, friends, and mentors—sometimes all in one person. I say that thinking of Rick Boryszewski, initially a business associate, later president of the company that hired and moved me to California. Mom called him "the father you never had, the male role model you missed growing up," and it's true. From Rick I learned how to be a man in business and in life: the key words being responsibility and accountability. Rick was a Vietnam vet, and the Marine officer in him came out often. I like to think I absorbed some of that too.

The list of people who inspired or empowered my push is too long to try to name. The point is that I also learned to pay it forward. A business consultant I hired once said to me, "I've identified your unique talent."

"I didn't realize it was part of the consulting project," I said. "What is it?"

He said, "Well, it's obvious: You get out of the way and let other people shine. You enable others to take the credit for their own ideas and efforts."

It's true I'm a behind-the-scenes guy. I like to see the job done, and it's a pleasure to see people around me rise to their best selves. Rick would say to people, "When your back's against the wall, call Mark. Don't get in his way or ask how he does it. Just watch, and he'll make you look great."

But I'll tell you how I do it: I work *for* people and *with* people. Because of all those who have helped me, directly and indirectly, I help others. As my career rose in finance, to do more I had to know more. I never aspired to be a financial analysist, for instance, but I became a Certified Investment Management Analyst. I never aspired to be a Certified Exit Planning Advisor, but I got the education. There are many more; I was always pushing, but I pushed because I cared.

In his book *The Gap and the Gain*, Dan Sullivan asks whether we measure ourselves by what we lack or what we've overcome. When I view the poverty in my past, I see how overcoming a deficit became my asset. It's no accident that Echelon Virtual Family Office supports entire family systems: financial, legal, and personal.

ECONOMICS IS LIFE

Economics is life; that truth I learned in college. Good finance is wise economics for individuals and families, that truth I've been living ever since.

About Mark

Mark Wade is Founder and President of Echelon Wealth Strategies, Echelon Asset Protection, and Echelon Virtual Family Office—companies that arrange and coordinate tax planning, risk mitigation and asset protection, wealth management, legal services, and business advisory services...for business owners, entrepreneurs, corporate leaders, and their families.

For more than 44 years, Mark and his teams—both local and national—have earned the trust and friendship of clients across the US: going the extra miles to understand, design, and apply custom solutions not just for investments, but for every family's unique needs and goals.

Mark's BA in Economics from Fairleigh Dickinson University launched a lifetime education, both formal and informal, including personal financial planning from the Metropolitan State University of Denver, and Investment Management Analyst certification from The University of Pennsylvania's Wharton School of Business.

When he founded Echelon Wealth Strategies in 1999, Mark had 19 years in financial services, leaving as regional vice president of a national securities firm. By then he'd added formal training to be a Master Registered Financial Consultant, Certified Asset Protection Planner, Certified Exit Planning Advisor, Certified Senior Advisor, Certified Income Planner, certified in Blockchain and Digital Assets, and an Advanced IRA Rollover and Distribution Expert.

Currently a state representative for The Wealth Preservation Institute, Mark has also served The International Association for Financial Planning, National Society of Public Accountants, Institute of Investment Management Consultants, Investment Management Consultants Association, Society for Financial Awareness, and the National Society of Financial Educators. He's also served on boards for local and national non-profits.

In 1992, Mark won the main event at The Grand American World Trapshooting Championships. He set two world records: one for the largest field—4,562 shooters—and one for winning by two targets, and with the only perfect score of 100. (Until Mark, every win had been by one target or a tie.)

CHAPTER 15

IT'S NOT THE MOUNTAINS WE CONQUER

BY JULIE MEATES

The highest mountain in the world is Mt. Everest, in the Himalayas. The first human to stand atop it was a New Zealander named Edmund Hillary, and what did he say about his world-altering ascent?

He said, "It's not the mountains we conquer but ourselves."

Not the mountains but ourselves... Whether the aim is a world record or to survive another day, whether the climber is a media star or a face in the crowd, if Hillary is right then we are surrounded by heroes at breath-taking heights.

Who are these unsung ambassadors of hope? The answer skips across a broad field. They are business leaders able to combine profit and human good...parents who climb or ride alongside their children in healthy, respectful ways...adult children lovingly caring for parents and grandparents in their twilight years...hospital patients in pain and uncertainty...nurses serving them, especially during covid times...kids in harsh homes... students with dreams...refugees learning to survive in foreign cultures. They are 'ordinary' athletes challenging themselves to set personal records. They are citizens of the world caring for the environment, giving earth a shot in the hopes of saving our planet.

And how is it that life's grandest and highest adventures are within our own natures? Because we humans will fall short. We hit walls, make mistakes, and choose poorly. And still we are made for heights. The grand adventure is our freedom to choose—sometimes by the quarter hour—to take on the mountain, or to stay on it, whatever that mountain is. And the great paradox is that any difficulty, any challenge, any mountain, is a gift: a chance to drive our spikes into What Matters, to learn and adapt as we go, to value the people who help us, and, as possible, to pull other people up with us.

It's no accident that the Chinese symbol for 'crisis' combines the pen strokes for 'danger" and for 'opportunity.' The stories below bear both strokes.

A CRISIS WILL BE THE END OR A BEGINNING. WE DECIDE.

During the COVID lockdown in 2020 when a bicycle ride meant sanity as well as exercise, a New Zealand athlete—one whose very name symbolizes victory—hit loose gravel and went down *hard*. Around him places of business stood like so many empty boxes. Good Samaritans were in their neighborhoods, sheltered in place. And there he lay with a broken hip and leg. Hours later he lay in a hospital room, isolated and overlooking the Port Hills. Suddenly, he had ample time to reflect not just on roadway hazards but on what it means when our independence spins out and crashes.

Our health, our well-being, tie closely to our relationships. Both are like glass balls that can shatter and break; both require constant vigilance modelling kind words, not critical harsh words. As the athlete's recovery cycled him now through surgeries and rehab, medical experts steered his course. His family, kept away by COVID restrictions, supported him from afar. And slowly, fitfully, a wounded man's internal climb took him from street to hospital bed to crutches to swimming 3.8 km, biking 180 km, and running 42 km in an Ironman competition.

"I can serve my weakness," Francis Cabrini said, "or I can serve my purpose." Isn't that the guiding star regarding any obstacle in our path – whether a broken relationship, a lost job, loneliness, divorce, death, an illness, an accident, a natural disaster or lack of money? At ground level our mountain looks like more than we can take on. Then we begin the ascent, and it becomes our proving ground, and then our launch site—this situation that we can conquer as we conquer ourselves.

"If I have seen further," Sir Isaac Newton, the English scientist, famously said, "it is by standing on the shoulders of giants." This athlete's view and progress expanded and sped by the giants in his life—medical, family and friends—because though we conquer ourselves, we can't do it alone.

Not ever. Edmund Hillary and Sherpa Tenzing Norgay stood on the highest point in the Himalayas with the aid of 362 porters and 20 Sherpas bearing 10,000 pounds of baggage. (Hillary did his best to serve those who had served him with such hospitality in their common home—building schools and hospitals in Nepal—working to protect the environment for future generations.)

A person averages 60,000 thoughts a day, by the way. Some days we conquer our cliffs and heights a thought at a time, choosing to replace despair with hope, reframe difficulty with resolve, visualize again and again what we want to see happen. The book *Atomic Habits* is a catalyst to 'atomic actions of hope.' Luke reminds us that even a one percent improvement every day can unlock 'the prison of the mind,' helping us fulfil our hopes and dreams.

WHAT YOU DO IS NOT WHO YOU ARE.

In Christchurch, Canterbury in New Zealand, young Hannah Glen—tall, beautiful, elegant—is a rising netball star. Netball is played much like basketball in the US. In New Zealand, it's one of the most popular women's sports, and in 2022 Hannah was on a roll: selected to the elite-level annual NZ netball tournament, nominated the region's netball young sportswoman of the year, and Christchurch's Rookie of the Year.

Then came the headlines: 'Horrible News for Tactix.' Shooter Hannah Glen, captain in Christchurch, tore her ACL at the country's Open Championships, ending her 2023 season before it started. Across Christchurch the gasp was audible: Hannah's injury didn't just close her playing season; it might end her game. But a seeming end instead led Hannah up a mountain to a grander view of true happiness.

In her year of healing, as she set new goals in achievable steps, Hannah was also climbing her internal mountain. Easing from the surgery on her body, she moved mentally from limited beliefs to grasping the power of the mind guided by positive thinking and gratitude.

Aren't we all like Hannah before her accident? How easily we wrap our identities in public praise, unsure who we'd be if those things were stripped from us. Hannah's challenge is our challenge because however great the gift or talent or skill, when a talent becomes an end in itself, it threatens to end the self.

WE CAN BE BIGGER THAN OUR CIRCUMSTANCES.

Lema Shamamba is one of millions of refugees from the Democratic Republic of the Congo (DRC). The day she fled her home country for the border, two of her children were in school.

Her five-year-old was at home with her. Sometime before, killer militia and rebel groups had invaded her village, and her protests made her a target. Lema and her young son walked for hours and eventually crossed into neighboring Uganda.

Suffering is an open invitation to hatred. We know that. The suffering isn't fair. The activities are illegal. Everything is *wrong*. Lema's husband's murder left her with three children and no home. When mercy is nowhere to be found, a person wants to slide into despair.

But Lema chose another way. In a humanitarian and environmental crisis she took on her mountain, believing she could somehow claim new ground and make a difference for other lives. Her country, the DRC, has the second-largest rainforest in the world. The 'lungs of Africa,' (it's called one of the lungs of the world), because its rainforest absorbs more carbon than the Amazon. Lema's small village was also rich in minerals. Now it became a site for large multinational companies to mine a rare earth mineral called coltan (short for columbite-tantalite). More than 7 million people died in the murderous rampages for technology-fed 'conflict minerals.' The DRC haemorrhaged refugees.

Have you ever had to face and overcome insanely difficult circumstances? In the camp where Lema and her three children lived, while some descended into hate, Lema stayed alive in every sense. She is an artist, a documentary filmmaker, an international speaker, a teacher, and the founder of Women of Hope. She is also gifted in embroidery. A stitch at a time, she works her needle in and out, telling on cloth her harsh truth, but always with hope. Her children now are global citizens carrying her hope and forgiveness, more threads toward mending a torn world.

We can gaze at heroes in the media, or we can learn to find the heroes among us, the ambassadors of overcoming. Not Batmen and Wonder Women, but daughters, sons, nieces, nephews, mothers, fathers, and brothers—lights leading us in ordinary times with their extraordinary climbs.

Heroes, by the way, are both made and born. In several of the previous stories, the subjects know sports and international success. Greatness is in their DNA, not just in rugby or netball, but in the way their Nana got up at 4 a.m. to milk cows before school—or pulled turnips, helping on the farm before netball practice. Another member in the family, Lauren Robb, recently ran, cycled, and kayaked 243 kilometers through an alpine pass, climbing 1,656 meters not just to conquer herself, but within a team determined to conquer environmental ignorance in an epic coast-to-coast journey.

Sports connects us in society, even in times of tragedy, as a diversion from everyday stress. "It has the power to sooth heartbreak and suffering," wrote US basketball referee Bob Delaney, "to express our hope...our wish to see ourselves triumphant." Like artists, musicians and other leaders, sports figures become stand-ins for our dreams. "We in the world of sports have a special calling," Bob said, "to use our power to help others to be a positive force in our country in times of need."

In sports, in war, in any part of life, life is teaching them to see the mountain for what it is: an invitation to go higher. And they know to seize the invitation.

"Until one is committed there is hesitancy," Scottish mountaineer W.H. Murray wrote in the book of his Himalayan expedition. But the moment one commits: "All sorts of things occur," he wrote, "to help one, that would otherwise never have occurred."

That's another point: the decision to climb is ours alone but we don't do it alone—*and we can choose to benefit others on the way.*

"I have discovered the secret," said the great Nelson Mandela, "that after climbing a great hill, one only finds that there are many more hills to climb. I have taken a moment here to rest, to steal a view of the glorious vista that surrounds me, to look back on the distance I have come. But I can only rest for a moment, for with freedom comes responsibilities, and I dare not linger, for my long walk is not ended."

Like Mandela, climber W.H. Murray wrote during extreme times of challenges. He spent three years in prisoner-of-war camps in World War II, where he wrote a book on toilet paper, the only paper available. His captors found and destroyed it, and he wrote it again. That book published in 1947, and its sequel, are credited with inspiring the renaissance in mountain climbing, Murray did not summit Everest, but some literature claims his 1951 climb mapped a route that that Edmund Hillary used two years later.

W.H. Murray, Edmund Hillary, Tenzing Norgay, and the many people with them learned on actual mountains what the rest of us learn on our bicycles, on ball courts and fields, in our businesses, even in refugee camps – to accept the invitation and take the climb.

Whatever your mountain, Murray would urge you to take it on. *"Whatever you think you can do or believe you can do, begin it,"* he wrote. *"Action has magic, grace, and power in it."*

About Julie

Julie Meates is a New Zealand-born humanitarian endeavouring to bring more peace, kindness, and love into our world. Her career has been multifaceted and varied. For her, family has been important. She is married with three wonderful children and a wide, diverse, extended family.

Julie has a passion for education and health, starting her early career as a teacher. She has also qualified as a social worker, counsellor and is now a barrister and solicitor, and is currently involved in post-graduate work in education and health. She is passionate about community wellbeing and has worked in a volunteer capacity in many roles – with the mantra and hope that kindness will be paid forward.

In 2002, she was the co-founder of the Fulfil A Dream Foundation with a vision of strong and happy families, strong and vibrant communities, and wise and visionary leadership – empowering individuals, families, and communities. Fulfil A Dream Foundation was fortunate to work with high-profile musicians, sportsmen, politicians, community, education, and health leaders. Julie was also the chairperson of a Maori learning centre (indigenous Kohanga reo).

Julie is a four-time Best-Selling Author. She has co-authored *Pay It Forward* with Brian Tracy, *Success, The Soul of Success – Vol. 3* and *Turning Point* with Jack Canfield (creator of *Chicken Soup for the Soul* series). All proceeds of these books are being donated to a variety of causes, including nonprofits that are leading the way to end human trafficking and modern-day slavery among other things. She is also a Certified Canfield Trainer. Julie is also a Producer on *The Truth About Reading* documentary with DNAFilms, the *Dickie V* documentary, *It's Happening Right Here*, and *Tactical Empathy*.

Julie has been featured on NBC, ABC, CBS, and FOX affiliates across the USA and television shows such as *Hollywood Live, Times Square Today* and The Global Entrepreneurship Initiative's Summer Symposium at Carnegie Hall in New York City.

Currently, Julie is a volunteer with community law's programme of community justice panels. The Community Panel process aims to repair the harm caused by the offender promptly, using restorative justice processes. She has been a volunteer on the United Nations executive in her Canterbury region as Board Secretary, and presently with the inception of Women of Hope Wake Up and Help Ourselves Trust Board.

Julie has been involved over the years with Women's Refuge and several other NGO and charitable institute organisations – COGS (Community Organisation Grants Scheme). She was vice president of the International Community Organisation (Wairarapa International Communities Incorporated) Society and was involved in community radio doing local, national, and international broadcasts. She has also worked with the homeless nationally and internationally.

Julie has been part of many community-led initiatives to strengthen communities in sometimes complex situations, weaving together storytelling and music, and empowering youth and community talent.

She has represented sport and has coached at high school, as well as being a physical education and health teacher and tutor, and she has further qualifications in design. In her high school, she was awarded best all-round person.

Julie Meates is a quiet leader, able to inspire, influence, coordinate and empower people to achieve desired goals. Julie is experienced in working in partnership with organisations, with local communities and individuals, to make a difference. She is empathetic, positive, non-judgmental and kind, with an ability to relate to a wide range of people.

CHAPTER 16

YOU CAN ~~NEVER~~ GIVE UP

BY LARRY KOZIN

~~NEVER~~ GIVE UP

I was six years old when my parents divorced and my mother brought home a new husband who terrorized my sister, my brother, and me. We all suffered, but as the oldest child, I took the brunt of it, both physical and psychological. I was fourteen when Dad rescued me, but the nightmare years had done their work. By the time I was in a dorm at the University of Michigan, my major in drugs, alcohol, and gambling—and the hangovers—made it impossible to get to class.

The spoiler alert is that on February 2, 2023, I celebrated seventeen years of sobriety, but the story of what made me who I am today is worth the telling.

When I was sixteen years old fate entered my life in the form of a job at a furniture store. I was brought on to unload trucks, which I hated, but when the showroom floor filled up, the boss had me help with sales, and there I excelled. Guiding customers through preferences and prices beat hefting dining tables and bedroom sets any day.

In 1976, with a perfect record of no classes attended, I dropped out of the University of Michigan to become a full-time furniture salesman. The upside is that I worked my way into a prestigious chain with premiere national sales training. Newbies like me were paired with seasoned mentors and put up against top producers. The downside was the prevalence of sports betting at work. At age nineteen, I was in with hardcore bookies, wagering fat rolls of money that I didn't have, strapped onto a financial, emotional rollercoaster.

Once after a big NFL weekend, my bookie rolled up in a new Cadillac to hand me my winnings in a paper bag full of hundred-dollar bills. By the next weekend I'd lost all of it at the racetrack and tried to recoup by betting higher sums on credit. Owing a thousand dollars or more, and with my bookie's threats ringing in my ears, I bought a one-way ticket to Los Angeles and bolted.

This was before two clicks on a computer could track a person anywhere in the world. When my plane touched down in sunny CA, as far as anyone knew—anyone including me—I was in a foreign country. Day one I found a fleabag motel room downtown and paid $50 in cash to cover seven nights. The next day I found a newspaper and a furniture store want ad for an experienced salesperson.

My Detroit sales training was as buttoned up and competitive as LA was laid back, meaning within ninety days I'd scored my way into management, heading my own store. I was also out of the hotel and in an apartment close to the store, driving my used car to Southern California's world-famous racetracks—Santa Anita, Hollywood Park, Del Mar. By day I made money selling furniture, and after hours I set fire to it. And sooner rather than later, the racetracks owned me, or rather the racetracks and marijuana owned me. Inside a year my indulgences won, and the furniture store let me go.

One of the guys at work matched my weaknesses for gambling and drugs, and we moved in together. Our work records lined up closely too, and around the same time we both became former employees and full-time gamblers.

My roommate was a more advanced addict than I was, deeper into the life and its patterns. Addiction typically ends in one of three ways: prison, insanity, or death. He began breaking into houses, and I let him convince me to drive the getaway car. I was too scared to do more, but I was no less part of the crime, and before the second break in, I wanted out.

Call it fear! Call it a spiritual awakening! By now I had enough driving citations—tickets, license suspensions, sometimes warrants for my arrest—to paper a jail cell wall, and I knew enough to want to avoid one. Years before, when I was sixteen years old, my grandmother had recognized my addiction and sent me to a twelve-step meeting, which didn't take, but a seed was planted. I wasn't a bad person; even then I knew that. I was a sick person needing help. The teenagers I see now in their first AA meetings break my heart, because they remind me of my younger self.

At the end of 1979, I walked into Gamblers Anonymous, and I knew I was home. GA has a famous list of twenty questions to help a person identify her or his gambling as an addiction. Did you ever lose time from work or school due to gambling? Has gambling ever made your home life unhappy? Did gambling make you reckless of the welfare of yourself or your family? A yes to seven of the questions indicates a gambling problem. I answered yes to all twenty. Somewhere inside me I also said yes to help from my fellow members.

I was in meetings every evening. I got a sponsor, worked the program, and my life began to sort out. I found another job in a furniture business, and I could feel God blessing me. I met my wife at work, we got married, and she got pregnant on the honeymoon. In 1982 we started our own furniture business, and it took off.

What a rough existence I'd come out of. At various times I'd slept at the Salvation Army or in the streets. Now I had purpose. Most important, I had two kids awakening a level of love in me beyond anything I'd ever dreamed.

My wife had come into the marriage with her own horrors from growing up, and together we committed to protecting our kids and our business. What we failed to safeguard was our marriage, and it predictably hit a wall. With few skills and no patience, more and more we found ourselves fighting at the tops of our lungs. Counselors got us nowhere, and seven years into marriage we ran up the white flag. Divorce is never positive, but even our kids welcomed the change. And in the peace, eventually we could become friends.

Not all change was positive. As a newly single man short on social skills, like an underground river finding the surface, my alcoholism erupted and flowed. Addiction is a disease of denial, and that also ran deep in me. Sixteen years would pass before I could see who I was.

Though I managed to avoid jail, the first of two DUIs sent me to AA, but I was still resistant. I never hurt or killed anyone on the road, thank God, but the absence of repercussions added to my denial. I could say to myself, "I'm not as bad as *those* people."

During that time, a doctor in a regular checkup diagnosed me with Hepatitis C, an incurable disease of the liver. He warned me never to drink again—not even a glass of wine with dinner, he said—but I ignored him. There was no cure and I'd die anyway, right? Before long, a binge would leave me so physically deteriorated I'd need two or three days just to get out of bed to drink again.

During that dark time I also married twice, each time to foreign women, each time for short periods. The first time was to a Swiss woman I met in a bar on her vacation to the US, a relationship that got me to Las Vegas. For the second, I flew to Colombia and chose a picture in a catalogue—an immigration-fraud case in the making, as her boyfriend was already in the US.

In December 2005, single yet again, I met a woman in Las Vegas, and we fell in love. I was in the throes of alcoholism, drinking before our dates to calm my nerves. When I was ready to propose, I bought a ring and took her to Mexico, but needing to calm my nerves, I binged, blacked out, and broke up with her.

Very soon after that, on February 2, 2006, I gave up, walked into an Alcoholics Anonymous meeting, and began my happy ending. A week later, Angie and I were back together. Seventeen years later our life together—with three grandchildren we adore, and ample financial means—continues to amaze me.

Maybe addiction is in my DNA. Both of my grandfathers gambled, as did my father. I also believe childhood trauma can cause addiction. I'm no different than any other addict; I became one, but I also believe God and the program can restore a person to have a beautiful life.

If you're sitting down, I'm also grateful to be an addict. If it weren't for the pain and misery I brought on myself, I wouldn't have this life now, beyond my wildest dreams, waking up every day to do the next right thing.

Several years back the medical world found a safe and painless cure for Hepatitis C. Instead of a transplant or the sometimes-deadly treatments at the time, for six weeks all I did was take a pill a day. The virus is gone, and my liver has regenerated.

An alcoholic is his own disease, poisoning himself with every swallow, living with no happiness, no joy, no peace, no hope. I never tried to end my life, but I considered it. I live in Las Vegas now, the city of casinos and suicides—the part the advertising leaves out. But the other side of addiction is hope, and Vegas also has more recovery meetings per capita than any city in the US.

Addiction is full of contradictions. It's a selfish disease and yet I'm here because of the recovering addicts who were willing to help me. Addicts stay sober by helping other addicts; whether or not the other one is ready to give up, helping helps us.

I say, 'give up'…for an alcoholic the better term may be 'surrender.' Just as a cancer patient needs medical help, an alcoholic needs spiritual help. The 'give up' piece is to surrender your ego, the part of yourself that only hurts yourself, and let God restore you to sanity.

That's where 'never' comes in.

You never regret it.

About Larry

Larry Kozin is passionate about his love of family, business and helping others succeed. He is the Founder of dozens of companies, including, but not limited to: MainStreetChamber of Commerce, Relationship Generation, Advanced Licensing, KozyFurniture, iDealFurniture, PerfectDreamer Mattress and Final Mile Technologies, to name a few.

His companies have made the INC 5000 list three out of the last five years.

Larry recently forged a partnership between Kathy Ireland and his ex-wife, Carol Russo, to be the exclusive distributor for a line created by Carol called Kathy Ireland Kids, with plans to open hundreds children's furniture stores throughout the United States, and simultaneously fighting to prevent child sex slavery with their partnership with Operation Underground Railroad.

Through these involvements and putting his life experiences and skills into practical application, Larry has built sales teams in the thousands in multiple organizations. He also is the inventor of the world's first furniture vending machine, called KozyVEND that is sweeping the nation.

Today, Larry is excited to keep broadening his horizons and growing through helping others. Showing individuals how you can blend spirituality with business ownership and create multiple streams of income with better results in less time, is the foundation of much of his work—as well as what allows him to be involved in so many opportunities. He is also a co-author for the best-selling book, *Cracking the Code to Success*, with renowned author and sales expert Brian Tracy, as well as a co-author with Dick Vitale on *Never Give Up!*

Larry currently resides in Las Vegas with his soulmate, Angie, and loves spending time with his amazing grandkids; Stella, Kane and Kobe.

Contact Larry at:

- Email: LarryKozin@gmail.com
- LinkedIn: https://linkedIn.com/in/LarryKozin
- Twitter: https://twitter.com/millionairZclub
- Website: https://LarryKozin.com

CHAPTER 17

THE FREEDOM TO NEVER GIVE UP

BY KEVIN HODES

Halftime energy erupted across the sold-out arena as a choir of children sang the national anthem and friends of the military laid roses to honor fallen soldiers. In the stands, dark blue veterans' hats dotted the crowd. At center floor, active servicemen and women stood at attention.

"Good evening, and welcome to Military Appreciation Night!" I began. These words I'd said for more than a dozen annual celebrations now, sponsored by Swypit, benefiting Folds of Honor and The American Fallen Soldiers Project. Tonight, I would also make this national event personal to my life.

Once a year at the Comerica Center in Frisco, Texas, my company, Swypit, leads a massive salute to service members and their families. The Folds of Honor Foundation gives college scholarships to the spouses and children of fallen or disabled military and first responders. The American Fallen Soldiers Project presents portraits to Gold Star families. Where better than at a Texas Legends basketball game with spirits already through the roof?

Twelve years earlier, the president of the Texas Legends, Malcolm Farmer, had asked Swypit to sponsor an event to honor the US military. "That's an easy yes," I said to him. Since 9-11, the military had moved to front and center in my regard. But my 'yes' depended, I said, on our getting to present portraits to families of fallen soldiers center court at halftime. Mr. Farmer said yes, and we proceeded to do it for many years, most memorably to the family of 'American Sniper' Chris Kyle (the first recognition, Chris' father said, to the entire Kyle family). Just google it, 'Swypit Chris Kyle' and see for yourself.

Now from the microphone I wanted to draw a short, straight line from the US military to my life. "When I was eighteen years old," I began, "and in my first semester of college, training to be a professional chef, I crashed and totaled my car."

Wait…a car accident? If that seems out of context to a 'never give up' military salute, stay with me. Because our military goes into extraordinary circumstances, I can have ordinary problems. Because certain men and women follow orders, the rest of us are free to follow our dreams.

Without a car, I told the crowd, I had no way to get to my college classes or to the four jobs I worked to pay for them. Dad was a blue-collar guy. At my age, he'd joined the Navy. Now as I sat in his living room, his advice was for me to "pick a branch and sign up."

But I'm building a career, I pleaded with Dad. I wanted to be a chef—to work in food service in all its varieties, and I was good at it. The instructors in my major at SUNY Sullivan were also top chefs at the world-renowned Culinary Institute of America.

Dad heard me that day, and he moved us to Plan B. He worked multiple jobs to make ends meet for himself and his family. Now he'd help me scrounge together $700 to pay for another car and finish college.

My mother and father divorced before I was old enough to have memories of ever seeing them in the same room. When they remarried to other people, my Jewish father's new wife was a Catholic who converted to Judaism, and they lived in Brooklyn. My Jewish mother married a Southern Baptist, converted to Christianity, and moved with him to Kansas City, with me in tow.

My stepfather was a mechanic for TWA, enabling me to fly often to see my father and his new bride, another thing I look back on with gratitude. On one of those stays with Dad—I must have been 11 or 12 years old—before dinner I said grace, thanking Jesus.

Right, Jesus.

"Where'd you get all that?" my dad asked.

"At Bible study," I said, adding that at my rural Kansas City home we regularly said grace.

That's all it took. I returned to Mom's house to find my things packed for an almost immediate U-turn back to Dad. The rush from rural Missouri to upstate New York may sound abrupt, and at the time I may have thought it was, but the move saved me. What Dad didn't know—and I didn't know to say—was that I was in the crosshairs of a sexual predator in the neighborhood. I would be grown, with children of my own, before I fully grasped the situation I was leaving.

But in my life, every 'crisis' has somehow also brought good. After their divorce, my parents moved states apart, for instance, but my place in their hearts went nowhere. Maybe it was my young age when they split, but instead of dividing my happiness, it doubled it. I grew up with two birthdays, two sets of holidays, two kinds of families exposing me to two worlds—far more than anything my friends had. "It must have been a pain for you," I've said to my parents, "shuttling me back and forth, weaving me in and out your plans. But it made me the man I am today, and I am eternally grateful."

Those years of adapting to two sets of circumstances did something else. They made me a hustler. By that I mean, in whatever situation I found myself, I hustled to fix it, improve it, or in some way supercharge it. My reflex is still to take anything I can to the next level.

When SUNY Sullivan handed me my degree, I was hired by Great Gorge Mountain View Resort—the old Playboy Club, in McAfee, New Jersey. My new salary helped me buy a Pontiac Grand Am, and the work was great until a fellow employee introduced me to drugs, grooming me to become a dealer too.

When the resort hotel closed suddenly, like my father whooshing me to New York, I was again pulled from a bad situation. This time instead of living with Dad, with my car and the shirt on my back, I collected unemployment and couch surfed/slept in my car in Jersey for a stint. Then I moved to my sister's couch in Brooklyn and a job at Pizza Hut. Next, with a $400/month apartment in the worst part of town, I was a full-time Pizza Hut assistant manager and part-time chef for World Yacht, cruising up and down the East River.

One day I was standing on West 23rd St. in front of a supermarket, still in my World Yacht chef's uniform, when a man introduced himself.

"I'm Francis," he said. "You a chef?"

"How can you tell?" I said with a chuckle.

"You at World Yacht?" he asked now. Francis worked on one

of the mega-yachts that docked next to World Yacht. This time, when I said yes, his simple response forever changed my life.

"Come work with me," he said. "Let's see how you do."

By now I'd left Pizza Hut to be assistant food-service director at Chapin, a famous private school on Manhattan's Upper East Side, whose all-girls student body then included Ivanka Trump. Through Francis, my first private-yacht cooking position was on one owned by Al Copeland of Popeye's Famous Fried Chicken and Copeland's Restaurants. There were others; and there would be a ride down the inter-coastal with Francis in a boat we docked and converted into a restaurant for the casino traffic in Mississippi. "Just remember you can always come home," my father said when I left for that trip, blessing me with the freedom to take risk.

About that time, my neighbor was trying to draw me into serious crime. This time I was rescued by leaving for a new chapter in food service, this time working on private yachts from Mississippi to Atlantic City, Florida, Maine, and Connecticut. Later worksites on land ranged from CNBC to a nuclear power plant. The final yacht I worked on—owned by the family of the original distributors of Coca Cola—led to meeting my wife, Sarah.

I proposed to Sarah on yet another private yacht I had worked on, the Mariner III. At my request, it was in front of the Statue of Liberty that I popped the question.

That was more than 25 years ago. Early marriage landed Sarah and me in Colorado in work that had me talking to business owners, which led to credit card processing. A friend in the business got me to Dallas, where I eventually opened my own business. What a ride. The world of credit-card processing is ripe for corruption. I work hard to infuse my business with honesty and integrity, which brings us back to the US Armed Forces.

My devotion to the military started not with Dad—though his navy years matter—but with my cousin Robert Hess, a fireman with Ladder Company 76. The Twin Towers were hit on his day off, and most of his unit perished. The next day, every fireman in the city showed up; Robert would be one of the first of them, years later, to die of the cancer that plagues those who served at Ground Zero. My Uncle Richie was there on 9-12 as well. He also died of related cancer.

Except for comedian Jon Stewart, who testified at Senate hearings, few prominent voices have sounded for the 9-11 heroes and their families. But I want to, and the reason for that is a mix of civilian opportunities gained and military lives lost. Since Swypit began Military Appreciation Night, I know hundreds of the personal stories of sacrifice among our first responders, our military, and the families behind them.

Many good programs exist to say thank you, and I urge you to serve through them—though any program should be vetted first. I choose to serve through the American Fallen Soldiers Project, helping families of fallen soldiers with comfort and healing and Folds of Honor with the gift of college educations.

Our men and women in uniform and their families embody the American spirit of 'Never Give Up.' Swypit is privileged to help acknowledge that. Year after year I tell my story, and year after year my words are a drop of water in what should be an ocean of gratitude because, "My Freedom Isn't Free."

Thank God for the men and women who never, never give up.

About Kevin

Since 1999, owner and founder of Swypit, Kevin Hodes, prides himself on bringing honesty and integrity to the world of credit card processing. Swypit provides much more than just a service. Swypit takes great pride in assisting their clients with growing and managing their business, while directly and successfully contributing to their client's profitability. His expertise in the merchant service industry is sought out and he has been seen on ABC, NBC, CBS, A&E, E! and Bravo networks.

In an industry that is rife with third party providers who are often more intent upon selling equipment than providing an effective solution for your business, Swypit ensures that their clients feel like more than just a number and receive an unparalleled level of communication and customer support.

Swypit provides world-class service, rates, and leading edge technology. In addition, they offer businesses free credit card terminals, assistance with point-of-sale systems capable of managing inventory, payroll, gift cards, as well as cash advance services. They also offer surcharging with no-cost credit card processing.

Kevin Hodes is a four-time Best-Selling Author and Executive Producer of the following documentaries:

- *Maximum Achievement: The Brian Tracy Story* — 2017
- *The Jay Abraham Story: Getting Everything You Can Out Of All You've Got* — 2018
- *The Truth About Reading* — 2021
- *Dickie V* — 2022
- *It's Happening Right Here* — 2022
- *Tactical Empathy* — 2022
- *Folds of Honor: A Fighter Pilot's Mission to Deliver Healing and Hope to America* — 2020

Kevin has received numerous Telly awards and the *Folds of Honor* documentary received two Emmys.

Staying active in the community and giving back is important to Kevin, which is why direct profits from Swypit go back into many community organizations, with his primary focus being 'The American Fallen Soldiers Project' and 'The Folds of Honor.'

CHAPTER 18

A TALE OF NO RETURNS

BY JUAN (CARLOS) SAMANIEGO

In my late teens I left the army and became an EMT and ambulance driver. I'm wired to help people. I worked long shifts and topped them with overtime. When a man at work asked me about all the hours, I told him I needed money for Christmas, and his next words forever changed my life.

He said, "Just claim 10 exemptions on your paycheck, and they don't withhold."

It sounded like advice, not cheating, so I did what he said. And sure enough, my next paycheck landed me in a spending bracket that my friends loved me for. I upgraded to a two-bedroom apartment and bought a new 1987 Nissan hardbody truck. By the next April 15, of course, I saw that paycheck deductions don't go away, they reappear as bigger tax bills. But I couldn't pay the bigger tax bills, so I skipped them altogether, leaving the exemptions on my paychecks and pocketing the income.

The IRS seemed strangely silent, but I should have known that, like roots in fertile soil, the case was growing against me, unseen, as a non-filer. The IRS knows where you bank, and sooner or later someone notices. Those were pre-computer days, and for me it was later, and when the day came, it wasn't the IRS who found me, but the State of California.

The Franchise Tax Board sent me a letter—standard practice—asking for a tax return. I addressed their request, but my days were numbered now. The state didn't notify the IRS right away. It took more years, and the anxiety almost did me in.

I get emotional thinking about it. To ask for help, I'd have to say what I was doing—or not doing—and the shame overwhelmed me. My friends? They'd reject me. I lived in silence, terrified, loaded with guilt, tied in knots.

Then I met Elizabeth. I was 35 years old, no longer a medic but a multi-entrepreneur. I had a network marketing business on the side, and I was making money. I also did taxes for ambulance people. (Oh, the irony.) When a friend at Chase Manhattan Mortgage told me they were looking for people, I applied, and even with no college degree, they liked me and hired me. More good money in the mortgage profession.

About that time, Elizabeth had her eye on buying a condo and needed to be prequalified. "Your friend Mariah referred you to me," I said when I called her, and Elizabeth promptly hung up on me. I called again. She hung up again. I called three more times, and, believing I was a spam caller, she hung up three more times.

Longer story short, after Elizabeth happened to walk into my mother's condo to see her floor plan, I called again. I said, "Your spontaneous home tour was with my mom. Would you like to talk about the loan?" When Elizabeth came to my office, I prequalified her for a loan and asked her to lunch. A year later I asked her to marry me.

This is where my guilt multiplies. My fiancé, about to inherit my financial life, knew nothing, *nothing* about my trouble with the IRS. Now the troubles on my horizon, and in my nightmares, were her troubles too. The IRS still hadn't reached out to me.

Why didn't I come clean? Easy: shame. Make that shame and fear of consequences. I told myself I could solve it without having to tell Elizabeth, but I was lying to myself and to her.

Before the wedding, I got online and googled a question: "Who can help me with my tax problems?" Turns out helpers came in three categories: attorney, CPA, or enrolled agent. Only these three could advocate for me with the IRS, shining a searchlight into the darkness I'd feared for so long. With a little more research, I decided to call Ernie Madison, a local CPA-enrolled agent formerly with the IRS. I found his name pre-wedding, but it was days after the honeymoon, okay, weeks, before I called him. I *had to* tell Elizabeth—*had to*—but when I did, I also had to have a solution.

The wedding was in November. In mid-December I picked up my cell and called Ernie, whose one available meeting date was just days before Christmas. His office was three blocks from our house, and I remember that winter evening almost as well as I remember my first lunch with Elizabeth.

I was expecting a numbers guy, a business-suited, black-rimmed-eyeglasses-wearing, pocket-protected robot of a person more at home with tax forms than human beings. Who else would be in his office so close to a major holiday? I drove up and parked next to a smallish building, got out and knocked on a side door. But instead of a guy in short white sleeves and green visor, the door opened to a 1970s hippie in a bad green sweater, his hair in a ponytail down his back.

"Carlos!" the man all but shouted. "Come in!" And he showed me to a seat at his desk. "Sorry it's so late! We're having a Christmas party in the building!" That explained the sweater.

I sat in the seat and told him everything: about my EMT work, the bad advice, how I dug a pit and jumped into it. I confessed my shame, my fear, the crippling anxiety. I didn't just weep,

I bawled, and Ernie listened. When he finally spoke, he said. "Carlos, you're a good guy who made a bad decision. Your part of the worry is over. Now let me worry for you."

For 15 years I'd carried a load of bricks on my shoulders. That night, for the first time in 15 years, I stood up without the bricks, straighter and lighter.

To start, Ernie would assess my situation with the IRS and catch me up with my tax returns. Owing isn't bad, he told me. Not filing can put you in jail. We formed a team that night, and days later, well after Christmas, I went to Elizabeth. As predicted, she was angry, but I also had a solution that gave us both hope.

Right off, I gave Ernie power of attorney, making him fully responsible to speak to and work with the IRS on my behalf. When you're sick, you don't call up and schedule a surgery. First, the doctor runs tests, checks blood, takes scans to define the problem. Ernie investigated and came to me with the words I'd long dreaded; but he also had a plan—that was the difference. "From eight years of unfiled returns," he said, "we've got to file for the last six. That gets you compliant."

A-h-h...compliant – squared with the law. The 'shame' quotient in my life was falling like mercury in a thermometer, or dropping like the ball in Times Square on New Year's Eve. New Year's Eve is the best word picture because this was a fresh start.

A taxpayer has to be compliant before anything else can happen. Ernie tracked down six years' worth of information and filed six years of returns—bringing me to the doorstep of resolution. I owed a lot of money, most of it penalties and interest, but a taxpayer owing more than he can pay, I'm glad to say, instead of going to debtors' prison goes into a 'currently non-collectable' category. For a time, that was my solution. Over the years the IRS would keep some refunds until I was cleared.

Financial relief was one thing. The biggest relief was in my head, my heart, my soul—and in my physical body. In my twenties, I thought I had a heart condition. As with my taxes, I was afraid to face the symptoms. When Elizabeth made me see a doctor, he diagnosed stress. Now that stress was ending.

One day out of the blue, Ernie said to me, "You're great with people, Carlos. You're empathetic. If you ever look for a career change, you should consider this type of work."

Was he crazy? I'd just emerged out of the tax tunnel of darkness. The last thing I wanted was to go back in. I stayed with the mortgage industry, but it didn't stay with me. In the 2008 recession, Chase laid off its workforce and I was back on my own. Still wanting to help people, at one point I trained to be a chaplain.

Bills don't go away, however, and I started back doing taxes on the side, and that brought me to a crossroads. "Hey, Carlos, real estate is picking back up," a friend said to me. "Come work with us." Elizabeth and I shook our heads. Not after 2008. We'd made a lot of money, but mortgages go away and so does real estate. But you know what doesn't go away? Taxes. Death and taxes. Or more to the point: death by taxes, which I knew well, and Ernie's words came back to me.

Why not help people the way I'd been helped? Not as an attorney or a CPA—but as an agent. To become an agent, I could get a college degree and work for the IRS for five years. Or I could pass three four-hour tax exams from the Department of Treasury, get my Enrolled Agent license, and build on my advanced degree in the school of life.

In those days, the IRS would send out massive books on all the tax laws. With a little research I found a shortcut named Eva Rosenberg, a.k.a. the 'Tax Mama.' For three hours a day, three days a week, I'd sign in online with Tax Mama and soak up training to pass the exam and become an enrolled agent.

It took nearly a year. Elizabeth and I struggled to support the family, always in some form of self-employment. When at last I took the exam, I checked through part one (individual taxation) and part three (IRS representation). Part two—business taxation—took three tries. Yes, three, until I passed and became an enrolled agent, and a one-time army medic, former ambulance driver, mortgage banker, entrepreneur, tax avoider of eight tortured years, began to do for others what Ernie had done for me.

The only way to take control of our lives is to take our problems head on. **Head on!** A few years ago I wrote a book called *How to Make the IRS an Offer They Can't Refuse*. Mostly it's about how people can solve their problems. The mafia have a word, *omerta*, meaning code of silence. Part of being in 'the family' is living a secret life. But secrets, like tax problems, only get bigger. And they have a way of coming out, sometimes with a vengeance. When I met the love of my life, the one thing that could destroy our future was my secret.

But finally, *finally*, the fear of hurting someone else trumped my fears for myself. I had to face it head on. The 'face-it-head-on' advice also applies to men of a certain age as health issues arise. Rather than call a doctor, we try to live around the symptoms. When it comes to relationships, the advice applies to everyone. If you sense a problem, *talk about it*. Don't avoid or ignore it. I give talks about taxes and relationships. The longer you wait to face something, the more distance and silence you allow, and the more likely the day that when you do talk, distance has already killed the relationship.

Bad decisions happen to good people. That's the bottom line. When I deal with my clients, I have only empathy for them, not judgment. The first time we talk, their tears flow just as mine did with Ernie. But the end of secrets is the beginning of relief.

Ernie is semi-retired now, in his 80s, and he's still my mentor—

in fact, we work together. His hair is shorter, though he's still a hippie at heart. He still hears from people needing help from a good heart and a sharp mind.

Most of those callers he refers now to me.

About Juan Carlos

Juan (Carlos) Samaniego is the Founder of Tax Debt Consultants, LLC. Carlos not only helps clients directly, but he also coaches and mentors other tax professionals around the country, including CPAs, EAs, and attorneys. His commitment to sharing his knowledge and expertise has helped countless professionals build successful careers in the tax industry.

Carlos is a member of the National Association of Enrolled Agents and the American Society of Tax Problem Solvers. His dedication to helping clients from all walks of life has earned him the 2020 Tax Professional of the Year Award, and an animated short film was created to tell his story. He was also presented with the EXPY award by the National Association of Experts, Writers, and Speakers.

Carlos Samaniego's expertise doesn't stop there. He's been seen on major news networks such as NBC, CBS, ABC, and USA Today, where he's shared his insights on tax matters. He's also made appearances on radio stations and news stations across the country, providing valuable advice to listeners.

Carlos was recently a featured guest on *Hollywood Live*. The show, which was filmed in Beverly Hills, CA, by an Emmy Award-winning crew, included guests from around the country who shared their expertise and stories of their success. Carlos was recently selected to be featured in an upcoming documentary on Viewpoint hosted by Dennis Quaid, which will be broadcast across the country on PBS television.

Carlos's journey from tax trouble to becoming a sought-after tax expert is chronicled in his book, *How to Make The IRS An Offer They Can't Refuse*. In this book, Carlos shares his personal experience and provides practical advice on how to avoid and overcome tax problems. His soon-to-be-released book, *The FTB Taxpayer Survival Guide: Navigating Tax Trouble in California with the Franchise Tax Board* offers practical advice and strategies for handling audits, appeals, and collection efforts with the FTB.

Through his Tax Debt Consultant Podcast and YouTube channel, Carlos continues to share his expertise and provide valuable advice to listeners around the world. His impact on the tax industry is undeniable.

Carlos takes great pride in being a devoted husband to Elizabeth Samaniego, who holds the esteemed position of COO at Tax Debt Consultants. He is also a loving father to his two children, Bella Samaniego and Andrew Samaniego. Andrew has distinguished himself as a graduate of the prestigious United States Naval Academy, and now serves his country as a Naval Officer.

Carlos also has a special place in his heart for his German Shepherd dog, Bruno, whom he adores. In addition to his love for his family and pets, Carlos is passionate about rescuing animals and supporting animal rescue organizations.

Learn more at:

- TaxDebtConsultant.com
- CarlosSamaniego.com

CHAPTER 19

WHEN I SAID I DO
THE BRENT AND SUSAN HAGGERTY STORY

BY BRENT HAGGERTY

Where do the subjects of potatoes, waterfront properties, and skydiving collide in one personality? In Brent Haggerty, if you know his *Gulf Premiere Sarasota* YouTube series, but it's *for* Susan Haggerty, if you know their love story.

Brent and Susan met in 1975 at the start of the school year at Nyack College, up the Hudson from NYC. Susan was 19, just off a plane from Dallas. Brent was a seasoned 18-year-old from Houlton, Maine, in the school cafeteria that day with his father and mother.

"Dad was to my right. To his right was this long-haired beauty, and I wanted his seat," Brent says, obviously telling a favorite story. "Dad leaves, I shift, and right away I know I'm over my head."

Make that head over heels. Three weeks later, he and the brunette were in adjoining seats at a movie called *Gone with the Wind*, for anyone there able to concentrate on the story. "When the screen went blank and I asked her how she'd liked it," Brent says, "she had to tell me it was just intermission."

On a Saturday afternoon in 1979, Brent and Susan received their diplomas; the next morning they were in church. Monday they rehearsed their vows at the church, and Tuesday they were back to commit for a lifetime.

Is this a happily-ever-after story? Mostly. Another commitment that factors in this story is the one Brent made in junior high when he promised to serve God, "wherever you want me to go." In high school he lettered and led in every sport, which spun his world in a few crazy directions, but by the start of college, God was back at due north. Susan had made the same promise for her life.

"My dad would say if God called you to be a preacher, don't stoop to be a king," Brent says. "Between that and my sense of God's call—and now this beautiful girl also headed for the mission field—we followed through."

In their next act, Brent 'squeezed three years of seminary into four,' working part time in a factory making Ziplock bags. Susan helped Vietnamese, Cambodian, and Laotian refugees relocate to the US, until nursing school came to mind.

"Nursing school?" Brent said. "You fainted when your dad needed open-heart surgery."

A sense of mission can change a few details. Cut to Susan with a nursing degree and Brent with an MDiv—Master of Divinity. Susan was six months pregnant with their first child and a floor nurse at Westchester Medical Center in Valhalla, New York, when Brent took a youth minister position at a church in Ohio.

Three years later, their vows to God and each other took them to France, where language immersion translated into nine hours of school a day, and then three months of practice on the Belgian border.

From Belgium, the Haggertys—now a party of four—moved to the West African country of Burkina Faso, literally 'land of upright people.' Make that 13 million people crowded into one of the world's most underdeveloped nations, where missionaries already there were overdue for help. The Haggertys arrived one day and started language studies the next.

If France had been a foreign country, Burkina Faso was a new planet. Conveniences were non-existent; help was scarce. Working in French, Brent and Susan spent the next two years paying 'informants' to teach them Jula, the trade language in this Pennsylvania-sized country of 65 official languages and widespread poverty and illness.

"The literacy rate was 14 percent," Brent says, then layers on more daunting statistics. "Half of the population had no healthcare. Life expectancy was 48 years. Annual income averaged $192." Eventually, Brent trained pastors at a bible school while Susan was a nurse and taught literacy.

Like most missionaries, the Haggertys came with high hopes and low immunities. Every Westerner struggled with malaria. Every missionary had near-death accounts. "I had Dengue fever and hepatitis too," Brent says matter-of-factly. "I didn't die, obviously, but there were times I wanted to."

Animals roamed the streets of Burkina Faso. People defecated in public areas. Open wells were easily contaminated. With their immuno-defenses under steady barrage, the Haggertys completed their first tour and went home on 12-month leave.

Destiny turns on small things. Early in their second tour, a toe infection in Susan's left foot refused to heal. When penicillin failed, an American doctor in Africa prescribed high dosages of the meds used locally to treat syphilis and gonorrhea. For Susan's immune system, that seemed to be the crowning blow, because after that the fatigue set in.

Nine-hour drives to doctors in a nearby country produced a catch-all diagnosis of Epstein Barr. Midway into their second tour, Susan was evacuated to the US. There would be one more stint in Burkina Faso, with Brent as field director and the Haggertys in a 'luxury' home with one air conditioner in one room, but in 2004, at the University Medical Center of New Jersey, a physician lifted the mystery. Susan's body was home to Inclusion Body Myositis, IBM, a disease marked by chronic, progressive muscle deterioration, and it was here to stay.

"Lou Gehrig's Disease—ALS—may kill a person in 24 to 36 months," Brent explains. "This is ALS in super slow mo." He and Susan cried all the drive home, then stood in the kitchen together "sobbing like babies until we ran dry of tears."

In the years ahead, falls would break Susan's kneecaps four times, requiring multiple surgeries. More falls added compression fractures in her spine. "It was like watching a horror movie," Brent says, "with the person you love in the lead."

The 'wherever' promise was intended to invite adventure, not muscle loss and broken bones. But if anyone ever told the Haggertys, as Job's friends told him in the Bible, to curse God and die, Brent and Susan were too locked in on the God who had suffered for them. For 24 years they served as pastor and pastor's wife at Stonecrest Community Church in Warren, New Jersey, and yet with every new fall, every new break, their future narrowed.

"While we still could, we moved to a better climate," Brent says simply, that being sunny Sarasota, near their daughter and her family, where Susan's scooter could navigate sidewalks any month of the year. This time 'wherever' took them 'from a pulpit to a single sermon,' as Brent put it when he and Susan left the pastorate. "And I don't have to take care of your mom," he added to his kids that day, "I get to."

A friend recommended real estate, and other people business, and Brent and Susan were back in language school, this time to speak finance, tax laws, contracts, and computers...to help out-of-staters assimilate into places called Sarasota, Lakewood Ranch, and Ana Maria Island. They were a team again: Brent fielding calls; Susan covering sales transactions; Brent driving clients to openings. Susan was also working a recliner/lift chair or transport scooter and typing with the ring finger on her right hand—the site of her only remaining dexterity.

As for the podcast, informed or tickled by his stories, people began calling the Haggertys from as far away as California, Massachusetts, New Jersey, Maine, and Ohio. "For a guy licensed for 18 months, we're gaining friends and making clients, and gaining clients and making friends," Brent says. To also make it personal, Brent added episodes like 'Blind Courage,' about a man with a seeing-eye dog, 'My Seven Worst Jobs,' from his own colorful resume, or 'You Should See What He Did for $100,' a lesson in integrity from his father.

In the midst of telling their 'never give up' story, Brent holds a long glance with his transaction coordinator. "She found 12 properties today that I'll go show tomorrow," he says. "We're listing. We're closing. It's hard to imagine two people who care more or will do more to learn, to get people exactly what they need."

Any regrets about the 'wherever' clause?

"One of my favorite verses is when Jesus asks what it would profit a person to gain the whole world and lose his own soul," Brent says. "Susan and I know how we define profit. We get to lead people to homes and, as conversations arise, to talk eternity. If you think about it, in three languages on three continents, we've always been in the business of helping people know God and enjoy him forever."

About Brent & Susan

'Last exit in the U.S.A.' That was the sign along Interstate 95 in his hometown in Northern Maine. But Brent Haggerty considers that exit ramp to be his entrance into the world where he speaks three languages and has helped people with life on three continents.

The most significant day of his life was in 1975, when on arrival day at college, he sat down at the cafeteria table, and was introduced to Susan Rae Lucas from Dallas, Texas. Four years of dating lead to graduation on Saturday, wedding rehearsal on Monday and marriage on Tuesday.

Brent and Susan Haggerty lived 10 years in Burkina Faso, West Africa, the 5th most poverty-stricken and under- developed nation in the world. Multiple bouts of malaria, hepatitis, Dengue Fever and other tropical illnesses were experiences which taught him perseverance.

"This is your disease, Susan. It's yours for life. It's progressive and medical science has nothing to slow it down or stop it." That diagnosis of Inclusion Body Myositis eventually took Brent and Susan from pastoral ministries in New Jersey to a Real Estate business called Gulf Premier Sarasota, (brokered by EXP Realty) in Sarasota, Florida. Susan researches the properties and coordinates the transactions. Brent just shows the buyers options and offers to help them navigate the process of sales.

Brent considers life to be 10% circumstance and 90% attitude. A never-give-up-attitude helps overcome every circumstance of life. The only loser is a quitter, says Brent. So until there is no more breath in the lungs or life in the veins, living out the promise of "In sickness or in health; for better or worse; when richer or poorer, till death do us part," Brent plans to NEVER GIVE UP loving the bride of his youth and living out the promise he made when he told her: "I do!"

Brent and Susan have raised three children and are proud grandparents of seven. This story is in their honor, hoping they will always persevere through any challenge life, health, marriage or finance brings their way!

For more information Gulf Premier Sarasota go to:

- www.brenthaggerty.com

CHAPTER 20

ONE POINT AT A TIME

BY NICK NANTON

His name was Floyd Fountain, and he was ancient.

Did I say ancient? I was fourteen years old and Mr. Fountain was sixty-five, maybe nudging seventy. He was one of the guys in my dad's neighborhood tennis gang, as quick as the others to step into a bedroom like Superman finding a phone booth and emerge in white shorts that were too short and knee-high cotton socks, ready for a pickup game of doubles.

I played in my share of those matches. By age twelve I'd kicked my last soccer ball and picked up my dad's love affair with tennis. The first day he ever whacked a fuzzy orb over a chest-high net, I can't say. What I can all but recite are the stories of his scrappy boyhood in St. Vincent and getting a handle on the game of kings. I tease him that going to the courts and back I'm sure he had to walk uphill both ways.

My brother and I were tykes when Dad moved the family to the US, tennis passion in tow. At first he played on public courts. In those years he owned a mattress and furniture showroom next to my uncles' electronics store in the Little Vietnam section of Orlando. One day they all got a chance to open the first Suzuki Jeep Dealership in Central Florida, maybe in the state. I was young, but I remember the excitement, the buzz. This was every immigrant family's dream.

For this immigrant family the dream came true. The showroom doors swung open, and the world beat a path to Suzuki Jeeps: smaller than their US counterparts, more affordable, better made. With success came the means for my dad and mom to build their dream house, which for most people would start at 10,000 square feet. Geoff Nanton was fine with a 2,400-square foot house; his dream was the tennis court 16 feet out the back door.

After that, forget country clubs. Never mind poker nights, Rotary meetings, hunting, golf, or stamp collecting. Weekends and time off, Dad was in our backyard with his cronies, swatting line drives, slicing the air—good men enjoying a good game.

About that time I was showing a little prowess myself. By age 14, I was competing statewide and the weekend warriors loved it. They were for me—like pride of ownership—and I felt it. I knew they wanted me to be all I could.

One day in a match, Floyd Fountain and I were behind. Significantly behind if you get me. In one of our walks back from the net, he said to me, "Nick, you know how to win at tennis, don't you?"

I said, "How's that, Mr. Fountain?"

He gave me that look through his 1980s metal-rimmed eyeglasses. Like initiating me into a natural law as obvious as gravity, he said, "One point at a time."

One point at a time. When it comes to life-defining advice, never underestimate simplicity. In the short run, Mr. Fountain's words put endurance in my game. In life, like teaching me the secret handshake, his words help me identify people worth knowing.

Not long after Mr. Fountain tossed me the keys to winning, I got a chance to test drive his advice on the hottest day of the hottest month in Florida. First serve was at high noon, and I can't overstate the heat in that one match lasting more than three hours. Thoughts of my state ranking, my tournament status, even of the end of the game, dried up with my sweat glands. But Mr. Fountain's words were in my marrow. *One point at a time.* For three hours plus, I played the short game, and at the end of forever I won the big one – parched, stooped, and mentally armed for whatever else was coming.

My company right now is producing a documentary about James Lawrence, a.k.a the Iron Cowboy. In 2021, James completed 101 iron-distance triathlons in 101 days. Translated: he knows the secret handshake. He holds the world record for consecutive long-course triathlons, and for the most half-distance triathlons (22) in one year. The 100-day idea came to him in 2020 when the pandemic shut down his livelihood as a speaker. The extra day he added for good measure. My company came to James' story in '22, meaning instead of going onsite to film his events, we inherited miles of footage. *Miles...and Miles!* How does a crew of mere human beings view, assess, and edit more than three months' worth of what *The New York Times* called "140.6 self-propelled miles"? Answer: one triathlon at a time, one sport at a time, often enough one frame at a time.

James speaks in terms of one step at a time, as in the weeks that he walk-ran the daily 26.2 miles to offset spreading pain in his foot, shin, and hip. He'll also say you push through the envelope because on the other side of impossible, more is possible.

A good friend of mine named Phil Randazzo is a civilian bent on serving the US Armed Forces. The staggering rate of suicides among servicepeople entering civilian life gives Phil a goal because entrepreneurship has given him purpose. While soldiers, sailors, and marines are still in uniform, Phil introduces them to entrepreneurs and shows them how to think like one. I've had the good fortune to join some of those events. A standout memory is Ft. Benning.

If you've ever seen a US Army Ranger, even one standing still, you know that specimen of mental and physical readiness didn't just happen. I learned some of that firsthand when the commanding officer at Ft. Benning invited Phil's team to join the Rangers' morning fitness routine.

When I heard the invitation, you know what I thought? I'll tell you. I said to myself, "I work out. I'm pretty fit. Sure, I'll give it a shot."

"Just shoot me" better describes my state of mind the next morning as I surveyed our course of twenty-five obstacles: six-foot walls, vertical ropes, and more sit-ups and pullups than the rest of my life combined. And did I mention a clock was running?

That morning thirty civilians with gym memberships came to the starting line, where US Army Rangers materialized alongside us. Some wore training packs; some were in full gear. A buzzer sounded, and . . . and cut to the end where three civilians crossed the finish line.

Why do I need to tell you I was among the three? Personal pride, partly. And because it draws a straight line back to Mr. Fountain in his metal-frame eyeglasses and trucker's gimme cap, knees flexed, whacking the racket on his palm, poised for the next serve.

Fifty yards into the Ft. Benning obstacle course, my objective had reset to micro-survival. The next situp. The next step. There were times, I confess, when my entire objective was my next or my final breath, whichever came first. When the commanding officer awarded three of us military challenge coins, the energy I gained from association with US Rangers could have lighted Las Vegas.

Something I haven't told you is that the years I was in middle school and high school competing in state tennis and playing with the weekend warriors, the Suzuki business was dead, all but shut down by a Consumer Report that my dad and uncles found hard to believe. By the time of those games on the home court, Dad's focus was on keeping his world together: going to work, paying the bills, covering our school and sports expenses.

In terms of achieving the big thing by taking on the next thing, especially when it's hard, I rank my dad with the US Rangers. What they know, what Geoff Nanton modeled, what Mr. Fountain put into words, what James Lawrence shows the world and himself, is that we conquer a challenge as we conquer ourselves. Again and again.

...One point at a time.

About Nick

From the slums of Port au Prince, Haiti, with special forces raiding a sex-trafficking ring and freeing children, to the Virgin Galactic Space Port in Mojave with Sir Richard Branson, the 22-time Emmy Award Winning Director/Producer, Nick Nanton, has become known for telling stories that connect. Why? Because he focuses on the most fascinating subject in the world: PEOPLE.

As a storyteller and Best-Selling Author, Nick has shared his message with millions of people through his documentaries, speeches, blogs, lectures, and bestselling books. Nick's book *StorySelling* hit *The Wall Street Journal* Best-Seller list and is available on Audible as an audio book. Nick has directed more than 60 documentaries and a sold out Broadway Show (garnering 43 Emmy nominations in multiple regions and 22 wins), including:

- Dickie V (Disney+/ESPN)
- DREAM BIG: Rudy Ruettiger LIVE on Broadway (Amazon Prime)
- Visioneer: The Peter Diamandis Story (Amazon Prime)
- Rudy Ruettiger: The Walk On (Amazon Prime)
- Operation Toussaint (Amazon Prime)
- The Rebound (Netflix)

Nick has shared the stage, co-authored books, and made films featuring:

- Larry King
- Dick Vitale
- Kenny Chesney
- Charles Barkley
- Coach Mike Krzyzewski
- Jack Nicklaus
- Tony Robbins
- Steve Forbes
- will.i.am
- Sir Richard Branson
- Dean Kamen
- Ray Kurzweil
- Lisa Nichols

– Peter Diamandis
……and many more

Nick specializes in bringing the element of human connection to every viewer, no matter the subject. He is currently directing and hosting the series *In Case You Didn't Know* (Season 1 Executive Produced by Larry King), featuring legends in the worlds of business, entrepreneurship, personal development, technology, and sports.

CHAPTER 21

THE SALE WAS A BONUS

BY RICHARD TYLER

The address had to be a mistake.

I pulled out the lead sheet and studied my Key Map for the twentieth time. Looking up, I scanned the struggling-class neighborhood around me for evidence of a house—any house, any evidence—in the market for a vacuum costing $500 before attachments.

I was 17 years old, in my best dark slacks and white button-down shirt, wearing a Sunday necktie and needing money for college. For two weeks I'd attended a course for vacuum cleaners sales training. For two weeks I'd role played, absorbed war stories, and memorized. I knew the fine points of fans, suction, nozzles, bags, filters, switches, dust, hoses, and cords. I could talk hardwoods, curtains, upholstery, and the varieties of linoleum floors. Complex scripts embedded in my memory could justify my company's positions on pivotal points like canister vs. upright. The fundamentals of vacuum cleaner science lay within my grasp.

But nothing prepared me for a weak lead.

If you know the movie *Glengarry Glen Ross*, you know it's

about a real estate sales office where the junk leads go to low performers and rookies. In those days, door-to-door vacuum cleaner sales were no different. Someone up the food chain figured if you could stick it out through a string of cold shoulders and slammed doors—if you could outlast the dead ends—then you got a real chance. The reasoning: Why blow a good lead on a quitter?

But why lose a salesperson before he or she finds their footing? Today, I understand that a manager of trainees can send out veterans and rookies together to benefit both. My vacuum cleaner trainer burned through a lot of territory not doing that. Paycheck-to-paycheck families seldom buy expensive appliances, and a salesperson learns to respect a real no, but our manager drilled into us that if for any reason we failed to even make the presentation, we were losers.

"You'll be a loser your whole life," were his words.

He said it to get people to stick around because sales, on the front end, can hold newcomers like a sieve, letting them fall through slowly. Our manager knew that, and he knew how to work the fear. He urged us to learn by selling to our families, thereby snagging a few sales from trainees likely to burn out before they could ever warm up.

There'd be no presenting to my family. My grandparents couldn't pay for my college, and neither could Mom. I was applying for scholarships, and the less money I had to borrow the better. This brought me to the help-wanted ads one Saturday where a long column promoting vacuum sales, well, sucked me in. Every home needs a vacuum, right? How hard could it be. I envisioned making $200 a pop, bonuses, and mass interviews. I'd pick up a couple thousand dollars locally in the next five or six weeks and take the work with me when I moved to new markets.

The scene shifts now to my first day of sales, alone in a rough neighborhood, lugging expensive equipment up concrete steps to knock on a screen door and ...

Nothing.

I knocked again louder, this time sensing movement inside.

At the end of an eternity, just as I knocked again the knob sounded and the door opened to a guy in a bathrobe, a big guy, who looked at me and slammed the door in my face.

No hello, just bam.

Like a robot I turned toward my car, my sales manager's voice in my head: "You'll be a loser...a loser...a loser."

On the sidewalk, it came to me that maybe I woke the guy up. Maybe he was surprised and didn't mean to slam the door, and I should try again. Pausing to gather my courage, I retraced my path and knocked, and after a long wait the big guy in the bathrobe appeared again. He shouted, "I told you I don't want anything!" and slammed the door harder.

My throat hurt and my eyes stung. Even my nose burned. I was 17 years old and had spent weeks preparing for this. I'd dressed the part and followed my lead sheet, and it was over before I could say my name. All I could see was my manager's face when I turned in the equipment and accessories with my business cards and Key Map.

You may be thinking I should have tried another door for a second call, but this was enough for a morning. No, for a lifetime. Still gripping the vacuum cleaner, I walked back to the sidewalk and to my car, where I got in and soaked.

I mean to say I soaked in self-pity and doubt. *Is this work for me? Is this whole thing a mistake?* So much time I'd spent learning every part of that vacuum cleaner. *Weeks*. What time did the sales manager come in, I thought. I'd need a way to drop off the equipment without running into him. There was no getting around Mom. What to say to her?

Then the revelation came to me. *Of course*. What I'd just experienced was a form of resistance that I now needed to identify. My mom and sister and brother and I lived with our grandparents. When I was a kid, and salespeople came to our house, where did they go? To the front door. But our friends and family, where did they go? To the back door, *to the back door!*

In retrospect, it was a stupid idea, but in the desperate reasoning of a 17-year-old on his first sales call, back door meant friend, and I needed a friend. I was humiliated and faced fresh humiliation later. I made my feet and body get out of the car. I picked up the vacuum cleaner and attachments, and I headed up the street as if to a new house. Once past the man's view, I made a hairpin turn toward his back door.

From a block away you could have heard my knees knocking and mistook it for road construction. My manager had a face, an expression, for people who returned their equipment without so much as a presentation, a sort of I-had-you-pegged sneer. I had to at least make a presentation. I walked the steps to the door. I raised my arm. My knuckles made contact.

The guy must have been in the back of the house because he came fairly quickly, still in his bathrobe, and the look on his face …he was motionless, unable to speak.

Who knows where the words came from, but before he could move, what left my mouth was, "Boy, am I glad to see you! The guy at the front door slammed the door on me twice! I'm Richard Tyler, nice to meet you!"

The rest of the story, as Paul Harvey would say, is a lesson in courage that I'd draw on many times over my life. The guy's shock could have turned to anger, but it didn't. He may have sensed my innocence. Maybe he saw something in me that he knew in himself. Whatever was in his head, it burst out of him in laughter, *belly laughter*. And with it—and this is a big lesson—every defense, every wall between us evaporated. For a moment we had a rapport, long enough for me to tell my story.

The big guy in the bathrobe invited me in and was nice to me, and I sold him my first vacuum. He was so nice that once I got past his exterior he bought every attachment—the ones to suck on the draperies, floor crevices...even the one to reverse the air to blow out with a paint spray. He bought one of almost everything we had and financed it all. At the moment I didn't care if the financing was approved. My part was done.

So on the day that launched my career in sales, the *sale* was a bonus.

As for me, I lived learn-ingly ever after. In college, the education I gained selling costume jewelry door-to-door to pay my tuition did more for my future than my courses. Down the road I'd build a corporation—my own college of sorts—to teach men and women around the world the kind of *never-give-up* lessons that started for me at age 17 when I learned to fear quitting more than rejection. The big guy could just as easily have said no, so it's not a story of how to make a sale but how to make a life.

Sales as a profession is not for everyone, but to cash in too easily at anything, to walk away when things get tough, will hurt anyone. That's the risk. For my part, I didn't stick with the vacuum business—didn't like it—but the lesson stuck with me that a bad situation has alternatives. Once I absorbed that, my world blew open. That handle on courage would serve me all the rest of my life.

One last time: It wasn't the sale I was committed to. Though I couldn't have said it at the time, I was committed to my future. What it looked like—its success quotient—had everything to do with what I did that day. Again, I didn't understand it, but I was committed to excellence.

I still am. To this day, in everything I teach, whether it be management, sales, leadership, customer service, or life, I implore people to remember: "Your success tomorrow is in direct proportion to your 'Commitment to Excellence®' today."™

About Richard

Richard Tyler, America's Corporate and Entrepreneurial Business Expert™ is recognized as the world's top Sales and Management expert. Richard is the CEO of Richard Tyler International, Inc.® as well as a diversified family of companies and services.

Richard Tyler is a Multi-time Best Selling Author, a nine-time Expy® Award Winner, a three-time Quilly® Award Winner, a two-time Editor's Choice Award Winner and a C-Suite Book Club featured Best-Selling Author. Richard is an award-winning Filmmaker, Producer and Director. His films can be seen on Amazon Prime, ESPN+, Disney+, Apple+ as well as other streaming services.

Richard has been inducted into the National Academy of Best-Selling Authors® and the National Association of Experts, Writers and Speakers™. Richard was selected as one of America's PremierExperts™ and his philosophies have been featured in *The Wall Street Journal, USA Today, Forbes* magazine, *Entrepreneur* magazine, *The Business Journals, Sales and Marketing Management* magazine, *Wealth & Finance International* magazine, *Acquisition International* magazine, *Corporate America* magazine, the *Houston Chronicle* as well as in hundreds of articles and interviews. Richard has been seen on FOX, CBS, NBC and ABC television affiliates, Telemundo.com, CNBC.com, Morningstar.com, Moneywatch.com, Wall Street Journal's MarketWatch.com, YahooFinance.com, CNN.com, BBC.com as well as other major media outlets. Richard is a member of The Business Journals Leadership Trust, an invitation-only organization exclusive to top business leaders.

Additionally, Richard Tyler has earned a worldwide reputation for his powerful educational methods, motivational techniques, and success training. His background in sales, leadership, management, customer service and quality improvement has allowed him to become one of the world's most sought-after Consultants, Keynote Speakers and Trainers. Richard has authored or co-authored over two dozen books with top experts such as: Brian Tracy, Mark Victor Hansen, Stephen Covey, Ken Blanchard, Denis Waitley, Dr. Warren Bennis, General Alexander Haig, Alan Keyes, Dr. John Gray, Ty Boyd, Dr. Robert Schuller, Jack Barry and many others.

Richard's recognition and awards include *Top Sales Trainer in The World Award, Game Changer Of The Year Award, International Sales and Management Consultant of the Year Award, Distinguished Speaker Award, Who's Who Worldwide of Global Business Leaders, American Biographical Institute "Man Of The Year Award" and Who's Who in American Education*, to name a few.

Richard's 6-Day Sales Immersion® Course has been considered the **Top Sales Training Program in the World** for over three decades. Richard's Leadership Mastery™ and Sales Immersion® Programs have been taught at the University Level for Executive Education. They are considered to be the 'Gold Standard' for Leadership, Management and Sales Education.

Richard Tyler International has been named the International Management Consulting and Sales Training Firm of the Year nine times and was also honored as the International Leadership Consulting Firm of the Year.

As Richard says, **"Remember, your success tomorrow is in direct proportion to your 'Commitment to *Excellence*®' today.™"**

If you would like to learn more about Richard and how he can help you or your business visit:

- www.RichardTyler.com

CHAPTER 22

WHEN A FALL BECOMES A LEAP

BY EMIGDIO ARIAS

This story starts with my dad.

I grew up in a small two-bedroom apartment in San Pedro, California, part of LA County. My two sisters and I shared a bedroom. One night as they slept, I woke up to a light coming from my parents' room. I slipped out of my lower bunk and padded down the short hallway to take a look.

My mom was under the blankets, sound asleep. My dad was standing next to the bed, dressed to leave for his job at a grocery warehouse distribution center. He had on his jeans, his long-sleeved t-shirt, his work boots, and a large industrial apron. He was exhausted. I was maybe four years old, and I could see that. As I watched him, still in his clothes, he laid on the bed next to Mom and closed his eyes, as if his soul was pleading for "just one more minute."

Five days a week, sometimes six, my dad got up in the dark to put in 12 hours or more at a job he didn't like. I know he disliked it because he said so. But he had bills and a family, and he did what he had to do.

That early morning in the dark hallway, standing barefoot in my Star Wars pajamas, I felt my dad's resentment, and it etched into my brain. I wasn't even in kindergarten yet, but I knew my dad was trapped. I knew I wanted more for him and for myself.

Thinking about this still floods me with emotion. I went back to bed that night with my mind racing, and that stays with me too. Even now as my head hits a pillow, it's full of thoughts.

When I finally fell asleep, the dream started. In the dream I'm walking near a steep cliff, and I stumble over the edge. I fall faster and faster, more and more terrified, until I wake myself up, sweating and breathless.

For a while the dream seemed to come almost every night: the cliff, the tumble, the terror.

One night, as I was careening down, I said to myself, "If this is going to keep happening, I'm going to enjoy it." My arms spread into two wings, and instead of falling, I flew myself to a safe landing. After that when the dream came, instead of waiting for my fall off the heights, I'd leap from the cliff and waft myself to the ground.

I was a grownup with kids of my own when someone told me that a dream is our higher consciousness speaking to us metaphorically. My dream was telling me—or I was telling me—to turn a fall into a leap. How that relates to my dad would come to me in moments and glimpses.

But first the irony. I graduated high school one year and got my first job the next year. One year after that, I was working to support a family. Boom. Boom. Boom. My first job came with no long-term plan, no plan at all—just me wanting some pocket money to not have to depend on my parents. But in three short years, with no plan of my own, I was trapped in someone else's plans for me.

Like Dad, I was working graveyard—11 p.m. to 7 a.m.—and like Dad I had a growing family to care for. For a blink of time, I had worked extra hours to buy extra things. For a blink, I could go out nights and weekends. Now everything I earned went to rent, utilities, and formula . . .

I was my father. As my wife and son went to sleep, I drove to work picturing him exhausted, lying down alongside my mom for one more minute. This was the life I'd vowed to leave, right down to the two-bedroom apartment. All the resentment that a four-year-old felt on behalf of his dad now I felt for myself.

Lack of sleep, meanwhile, can make a person edgy. One day at work I thought my supervisor was unreasonable, and I smarted off. He yelled back. I walked off...and the next day I was fired. Wait, fired? With another baby on the way? Sure, sure, I said I didn't want to be like my dad, but at least my dad provided. At least he had work to go to. I was over the cliff and in a free fall.

For a month the fall picked up speed, faster and faster. I believed my forehead was branded with a capital F. In such disgrace, how does a man go on? Any potential new employer would call my previous employer, who would say I had an attitude problem, that I didn't play well with others. My family was doomed to life on the street.

Earl Nightingale was a business speaker in the 1950s who talked about character and the meaning of life. Many of his writings are near legend now. Some people call him the father of modern business motivation. In one of his essays, he says if all the fog covering seven city blocks to a depth of 100 feet were collected and held in a single drinking glass, it wouldn't fill the entire glass. He compared the fog to our worries. No matter how much our fears expand to fill our heads, condensed they wouldn't fill a jar.

After weeks of self-loathing and self-pity, one day I broke

through the fog and said, "Enough!" I told myself I could stay in the house, unshaven, unkempt, marinating in self-pity, or I could get up and find work. I shaved and got a haircut, I put on my best interview clothes, and I went job hunting left and right. And I found warehouse labor, like the last job, that paid more.

In 1995, I graduated from high school. In '98, my first son was born, and in '99, my second son. From '98 through 2001, I had multiple jobs, each one better than the last—the final two as a truck driver. In 2001, my involvement in the labor movement led to my being a union rep—an advanced education if ever there was one, predictably full of political ups and downs.

In 2009, I had a bad political falling out with my boss and was let go.

I haven't mentioned my divorce. Problems in one part of life spill into every part, and around the time of the political falling out, my marriage fell too. I had no sense of purpose, no passion for how I spent my waking hours. All my divorce gave me was more responsibilities and less support.

Had I learned nothing about fear in a free fall? I was more afraid than I've ever been in my life, in part because this time the stakes felt higher. What employer wants to bring a former union representative into the company? Even an employer willing to entertain the dirty, ugly politics in the union, if he should call my previous employer—the union—he would hear ugly things about me. I was a loser. I was lost.

For a month, like before, I indulged in self-loathing and self-pity. And one day, like before, I got up and cleaned up and looked for work. Before the week was over, I was with another union in a better position at a higher salary. That education lasted six years, until I admitted to myself that union work itself was not for me. About that time, I also saw the words, "Leap and the net will appear," and for the first time in years the dream came back to mind.

I was done with the union rep identity, done with politics, but I was also depressed. I wasn't suicidal, but I didn't want to live. I went back to Earl Nightingale's story 'Acres of Diamonds,' about a famer in Africa who sells his farm for the money to go hunt for diamonds. When he fails at diamond hunting, he gives up and jumps off a mountainside. The person who bought the farmer's land, meanwhile, finds an interesting rock in a stream on the land and brings it home. A friend tells him that rock is a diamond in the rough, and the stream has thousands of those rocks.

The first farmer's dream had been on his own land all along, and maybe my destiny was already with me. Twenty years as a union rep had schooled me in organizations and reality, in labor problems and negotiations, in people, rules, challenges, cases, situations, precedents. I talked to a management consulting firm, which reviewed my resume and instead of calling me in two weeks called in two days. On a Friday I quit my union; on a Monday I was an active management consultant.

When I leapt from my steady income, the net appeared. Or you could say I was back learning to fly. Instead of falling, my income rose way, way up. So did my health, interestingly, and my happiness, which also spill into other parts of our lives.

I don't want to over-generalize, but when I was growing up, we were so busy telling kids to go to school and get a job to buy things that we forget to say, "Find what you love doing and do it to the best of your ability."

I tell my kids now—my two sons and my daughter—to go after work they can love. Somewhere in what they already love to do, I tell them, in what attracts their interest, lies their direction.

If I could whisper into the ear of my younger self, I'd say to that kid to leap sooner than later. Don't wait for the universe to shake up your world, I'd say. Shake it up yourself.

When I was 20 years old, I loved speaking in front of crowds. I was happy with attention, teaching, protecting, and helping people. Even then I enjoyed motivating people, lifting their emotions, making them laugh…and here I am, after many falls, learning to leap, to land on my feet, and showing other people how to fly.

For much of that, I thank my dad.

About Emigdio

Emigdio M. Arias is an Elite-Level Mindset Coach, Executive Coach, Prosperity Mentor and Personal Transformation and Thought Leader, he will help you or your organization achieve higher levels of success.

Emigdio is the CEO of Triumphant Mindset LLC, and the Lead Instructor and Trainer for The Talisman Society - Accelerated Self Improvement and Personal Growth, where he facilitates greater success for individuals and groups to get them from where they are to where they want to be.

For over twenty years, he has had a passion for helping and creating better leaders. He focuses on a transformational process, utilizing techniques that have helped thousands of people achieve their personal and professional goals. With a strong background in NLP, Success Principles, Hypnotherapy, and Time Line Therapy®, he provides personalized training that helps people gain critical insights, take risks, and overcome challenges.

An energetic, engaging presenter, and empathetic yet bold communicator, he helps improve communications at companies across industries – assisting people in discovering opportunities for personal and professional development, making organizations stronger and more capable of realizing aggressive business goals.

Professional Credentials:

- Certified Success Principles Trainer
- Certified Executive Coach
- Certified NLP Trainer
- Certified Trainer in Hypnotherapy
- Certified Master Practitioner in Time Line Therapy®

Emigdio M. Arias helps individuals and groups let go of limiting beliefs and release negative emotions—increasing productivity and happiness. He helps in goal identification and goal setting—providing creative, effective solutions to elicit transformative breakthroughs.

Emigdio helps propel people to define their purpose, take 100% responsibility for their lives, and take inspired action to go after what they really want.

Emigdio proposes:

1. Are you ready to take your personal and professional success to the next level?
2. Aim high. Go after what you want.
3. He strives to help people lead happier, healthier, and wealthier lives.
4. Connect with him today to accelerate your path to a Triumphant Mindset.

Contact information for Emigdio:

- www.TalismanSociety.com
- www.TriumphantMindset.com
- Instagram: @triumphant.mindset

CHAPTER 23

THE OTHER SIDE OF THE MOUNTAIN

BY ZACK VISCOMI

Why would two former Marines at Yosemite National Park hike nine miles up a mountain and nine miles down with no food, water, or map, on the day the park closes for winter?

In our defense, it started as a morning walk.

Brian and I were roommates in Iraq. Our wives are best friends, and our kids play together. He trains police officers now, and when a teaching gig came up in Central California he asked me to come along. We'd camp out, he said, and my wife, my amazing wife, gave us a green light.

Yosemite is a great valley floor surrounded by granite mountains. From the camping sites at the base it rises 8,000 feet to its Half Dome peak—8,000 feet through waterfalls, sequoias, and wildflowers. In its sane months, visitors enter a lottery for passes to hike to the top of the Half Dome, which sounds like a good day in nature, but the trail is still dangerous. A hundred times a year park rangers rescue hikers who misjudge the distance, the rigor, or themselves. Three years ago, a woman died coming down the steep final climb to the dome. A 19-year-old taking a selfie recently fell to his death.

Brian and I arrived on November 11, Veteran's Day, one day after the Marine Corps birthday. That night, our unheated tent fell to 10 degrees, and before sunrise we were up scrounging for coffee. Brian ate a biscuit. I may have had yogurt. Across the valley floor, the week-old snow had melted and refrozen into a vast walking hazard.

We'd swing up the John Muir Trail, we agreed, take in the first waterfall, and hike the Mist Trail back down through the redwoods. I wore jeans, my Timberland work boots, and a jacket with a little trail mix in one pocket. Our path was iced over but the day was young, and we had energy to spare. We reached Vernal Fall in half the time we expected.

On to Nevada Fall, we said, another breezy two-mile stretch to the top of the waters that slam into rock, exploding into cold mist. Brian and I took in the sight, and then we looked at our watches: not even 10:30. A pair of hikers passed us with claws and picks for the ice, and we shrugged. Why not hike on through the forest to the base of the Half Dome?

Now our lack of provisions began to tell. A mile or two in, I slipped and tweaked my right knee, something normally I'd walk off, but the night before I'd worked out with a former professional athlete, and I was a little beat up. Maybe it was the incline of the walk or my work boots on the slick path, but with every step the pain in my knee amped up.

Around us the woods loomed, beautiful and harsh. As the elevation rose, the frozen melt of the valley became snow sometimes two feet deep. Except for our steps, the only sounds were wind and falling ice. No more evidence of humanity. Phone reception was a memory. I limped, but we stayed on mission, mostly single file, slipping now and then, up to a Y in the trail. To our left lay the Sub Dome and, beyond that, as the guidebooks warned, the 'extremely strenuous' Half Dome.

THE OTHER SIDE OF THE MOUNTAIN

On to the Sub Dome, we said, hoping to get as close as possible to the Half Dome without permits or climbing gear. But a few steps past the Sub Dome checkpoint we both knew better. Brian had run the Marine Corps Marathon 10 or 12 days before. I needed no added distance on top of our long trek back. Not on this knee. Not without food or water. Our six-mile round trip was now nine miles one way. We turned, and with my first step downhill, an entirely painful jolt like an electric current seared through my knee and up to my throat.

On we walked, scanning for park signs, wishing the day was over. "This is temporary," I'd say to myself. "This is temporary." "This is temporary." Let permanent damage come, there was no quitting Brian, no quitting myself. Two miles down, at another fork, we met a ranger closing the trail we'd taken up, making us the season's final hikers on Yosemite's most dangerous winter stretch, and forcing us to take a new route.

All my thoughts had fixed on making it over the first route, and the change rocked me. A body's job, meanwhile, is survival; its alarm is pain, and my knee excelled on sounding the alarm, which my job now was to override. This isn't survival, I'd tell myself, it's discomfort. Calorie depleted and lightheaded, Brian and I walked on. A few times at higher elevations I'd grabbed handfuls of snow for hydration. Now the inside of my mouth felt like notebook paper. The debate raged between my right knee telling my body to stop and my brain promising that warmth, food, and water were eight hours away.

Twice Brian and I missed turns, forcing us to backtrack uphill to come down another side of a fall. Uphill or down, for both of us life had narrowed to every next step. The trailhead lay another six miles down. The sun would set soon. We walked single-file, up and down, mostly down, always on ice or snow, straining to supplant calories with willpower. My knee was raw, my feet were soaking wet.

From Nevada Fall south to Vernal Fall is a series of switchback staircases, hundreds and hundreds of stairsteps carved into granite. In the hot months, they're slick with spray from the falls. Now the stairs were paths of compacted snow, thank God, allowing me to sit on my left foot, stick out the injured leg, and push myself like a single-ski sled. Switchback to switchback we climbed and descended, climbed and descended, me sitting and pushing as much as I could, working to reach the trailhead two miles from camp.

Through most of the morning's ascent, Brian and I had laughed and joked. Now we moved in our own spheres of pain, every step more labored than the last. The moment came when we finally reached the trailhead, and Brian continued down the two-mile road to camp. From behind, I watched him move, a silhouette with a limping gait.

To this day I don't know what damaged my knee. What I know is that an extended hike in a large national park, beyond cell reception and human help, beyond choices, and beyond giving up, led me to the other side of myself. Brian and I both hurt. Neither of us could walk for the other, and neither of us would quit. Near the valley floor other hikers appeared, but by then the worst was behind us. Thirteen hours after we set out on an easy hike, we hobbled into our tent, changed clothes, and hobbled to the café for food and drink.

My mountain that day was my pain. *Failure is inevitable, I tell my kids, but quitting is not.* In the long walk down, to give up on myself or Brian would have let the negative voices win—the voices that in my growing-up years told me I was incapable, dumb, slow, not good enough. Through the forest leading back from the Sub Dome, on the switchbacks between the falls, and finally on level ground, the physical pain strangely mirrored the emotional pain I'd avoided for years. If I could walk on that knee and get home, I knew I could scale my past, and I have. Since that November 11 in Yosemite, with increased confidence I've moved toward my once-uncharted mountains of authenticity, honesty, exposure, and self-acceptance.

I say a lot to my kids. I tell them we have more in the tank than we think we do. I tell them the path to reward leads through discomfort. To take on a mountain, even in pain, is to permanently gain a higher perspective.

Looking back, what would I do differently? Not one thing. I can put my mind on what I failed to pack, or I can learn from the heights I scaled. A full day of unavoidable hurt now helps me help others with their wounds. Own the pain, I can say. Keep walking. Speak it, use it to build trust, credibility, authenticity . . . use it to climb higher and to get home.

Brian and I will return to Yosemite, albeit a little more prepared. I can't know what limits we'll face, but there's more in us than either of us know, and any negative voices are lying. We are good enough, strong enough, capable enough, smart enough. To embrace this truth is to take on mountains.

...And to know the sky's the limit.

About Zack

For over 20 years, Zack Viscomi has shown repeated success in leadership as well as business development, branding, operations, and sales. Zack has worked with hundreds of entrepreneurs and professionals all around the world in the development of their CoreStory as well as teaching the power of The Business Trifecta®, the proven system behind business growth, and providing the tools needed to live a life of Joyful Impact and Significance.

Zack is the President of Celebrity Branding Agency and Integrator of DNA Media. He is a Best-Selling Author and has been featured in *USA Today*. He has also been seen on ABC, NBC, CBS, and Fox affiliates around the country. As an Ambassador for the Global Entrepreneurship Initiative at Carnegie Hall, he presented on stage about the importance of story for businesses, and how we all have a story to share.

Whether it's developing new processes, hiring, training, and implementing technology to help a service and repair company post profitable quarters after continually experiencing net losses, or developing a system for the accounting department to decrease another company's receivables by over 70%, Zack is passionate about helping people succeed, while becoming the best versions of themselves.

Zack also enjoys mountain biking and spending time with his wife, Alli, and their three children, Scout, Aries, and Poppy – not to forget their two dogs: a boxer/ridgeback/pitbull mix named Miley, and a mini-pug named Mona.

Learn more at:

- ZackViscomi.com
- Celebritybrandingagency.com

CHAPTER 24

MAGNIFY

BY STACEY JOHNSON

As a kid I dreamed of going to high school in Dallas, my glory days. I'd have more freedom and do things like try out for the drill team. And then, right before my freshman year, my mother and her new husband moved our family hours away to the very small town of Childress, Texas.

They wanted us in a better situation, and in truth we needed one. My mom suffered through and survived multiple abusive marriages as a young woman. On Saturday mornings in our home, it wasn't unusual to step over a coffee table of marijuana and alcohol to get to the backyard. Mom's last husband had filled us with hope for a better life—he even adopted my sister and me—but when I was in the sixth grade, he sexually abused me. By the age of 12, I was familiar with smoking, alcohol, sex, and drugs.

Mom was 17 years old when I came along with no books on parenting, no motherhood tribe to guide her, and no model of nurturing and healthy love. My mom did not grow up hearing I love you; she didn't hear that from her father until she was an adult. I remember manipulating conversations, desperate to get her to say those three words to me.

After Mom's divorce, when she started dating again, she reconnected with a friend of the family. He was a Christian, and raised by a praying mother, who now prayed him and the rest of us back to his hometown.

The day Mom broke the news to me, she tried to soften the blow by giving me free rein in our last week in town. "Do anything you want," she said. "No questions. Just be ready to go on Saturday," and I took her at her word. My friends and I spent every waking moment together, partying nonstop, making it that much harder for me to leave. I cried for the entire four-hour drive to Childress.

In many cases, my tears were warranted. When I say Childress was diverse, I mean it had a wide gap among ethnicities and cultures. I was a little brown girl, half Hispanic, often mistaken for African American. Now I felt like a city girl in the sticks.

One weekend, my sister and I went to a festival at the town park. We wore cutoffs and crop tops, our hair spiked and sprayed '80s style. Our style met Dallas standards but the small town looks of disapproval were clear. The only time I skipped school in Childress, the one time, the principal called to alert my mom, my grandma, and my aunt.

My first friend in Childress was Jennifer Evans, a girl my age who invited me to church, which I was sure my parents or grandmother put her up to. And a day came when I was so bored I agreed to go.

I won't say Jennifer was pushy, but one visit didn't end the invitations, and 'no' was never a right answer. She made an intentional effort to hang out with me and make me feel welcome. On a bus trip, for instance, when she sweetly invited me to give my heart to Jesus, my words were, "Hell no! Why would I give away my control to someone I can't see? I take care of me. Period."

Jennifer took no offense and kept calling. One weekend at a Dawson McAlister youth conference, we arrived a little late to a scene of thousands of kids rocking to band music. Way up on the first two rows I could see a guy on a platform—a chair, maybe—his hands raised as high as they could go. His face was turned away, but he was crying and singing with everything in him, and I stared at the sight. In all my life I'd never loved anything like that.

A couple of months later, Jennifer invited me to a Disciple Now weekend, a string of mini-teen retreats in people's homes, where I recognized a few kids from one of my school classes—guys I was close to and liked to hang with. That weekend they talked about God in ways I'd never seen kids my age talk—more than just showing up and giving answers.

"Cool people do this?" I thought. "Imperfect people? Not just the prim and proper, sweet kind like Jennifer Evans?"

By now Jennifer had asked me twice to give my life to the Lord, and that night I couldn't escape two things: the unconditional love and the peace she spoke of. "I want to pray, and I'm not sure what it means," I said to her. "You talk about love and peace as if they're things I could know, but I'll take the risk."

Until then, I'd felt love when I made good grades or gave a guy what he wanted or helped stem my mom's depression—things weighted with pressure and responsibility, hardly unconditional. Until then 'peace' had sounded boring to me. Now I saw love and peace in people I'd want to know, and I longed for them too.

What was there to lose? In a child's bedroom in my friend Lance's house, Jennifer and I prayed. And people may doubt their faith, but since that night I've survived a cancer death sentence, years in a miserable marriage (trying to earn my mother's love and acceptance), an affair that blew up my life to get out of that marriage (says my therapist), and blow after blow of heartache and trauma. But I've never doubted God's love or my faith. It took a while for my behavior to catch up with my certainty, but on my worst days He's never let me go. Since that day in the bedroom, my heart has always been His.

That said, redemption can also cause disruption.

I was new to this small-town life, but I soon became aware that only achievement brought acceptance. And if the well-to-do had to perform, the rest of us had to dance five times harder to overcome our color, lack of family connections, or the 'you're-not-from-here' factor. My younger sister and I, so clearly not from there, could feel our rankings.

Other rejection, of course, was overt. In my sophomore year, I somehow landed in the high school 'Greenbelt Bowl' court—which was a big deal, causing some of the mothers in charge to wonder how I got there. Heck, I wondered, too. There, to my shock, the court of my peers voted me Miss Congeniality, I wanted to cry out: "Wait! You guys chose ME?" If I could be chosen, maybe I wasn't 'less than' after all.

At home my mom and new dad were building their family and active in church. I loved God, but the big new lifestyle, the new expectations, the small-town public scrutiny, they all made everything feel like a performance. Mom and I fought so much that I moved in with friends, a kind Hispanic family. That's when the Greenbelt Bowl mothers issued the new rule that a candidate for the court must live in her home, looping out only me, and once again, I didn't fit the rules for belonging.

That Christmas, my parents invited me to dinner at my grandma's in another town, and, wanting to belong, I went. Like the air before a thunderstorm, the house was tense with fears of my misconduct. And then it happened. My innocent joke to my sister set my mom off and then it was on. Trying to protect her, Dad stepped in. In a blur he and I were in the yard, me trying to leave, him coming after me, both of us yelling, arguing, wrestling. At some point I was pinned down so hard my teeth cut through my upper lip. The adults in my life didn't know how to handle me, and I didn't know either. All I knew was that I was unwanted.

Broken and on my own again, in the dark I walked away from my grandma's, my place of treasured childhood memories. I had no home, nowhere to fit in, no one to tell me why life was so damn hard, so full of hurt, no one to teach me how to cope or heal. A few houses down, I could make out that a woman on her porch was whispering loudly, gesturing to me to come closer. I stepped into her yard, and as I did, something inside of me lifted.

"I heard," she said, guiding me up the porch steps and into her living room. I could see she had Cancer – no hair, no eyebrows, her head covered. "I can't do much," she said to me, "but I can help you get to a bus or something. Where do you need to go?"

Who moves toward a teenager that the whole world shuns? I'll tell you who – a fellow sufferer – someone with eyes to see. Where my family saw an irritant and disruption, in her pain this neighbor saw my pain. Why couldn't my parents see that? In school, my teachers loved me. Why the tension at home? I know that answer too. Because first we're products of our environment, and then our environment despises us for being a mirror.

God alone sees us perfectly. When the people we want to love us fail us, He wants us to look up and see the gifts in those He's placed around us. We strive for audiences who aren't there, bending and contorting ourselves for people committed to agendas about us instead of for us. Those minds we can't change. That's when we look instead for God's unexpected presence in the ones He purposely places near us to help, heal, and love us well.

My sixth-grade teacher, Mrs. Bishop, was one of those people. No matter how bad it got at home, I was her 'Baby Girl' and she was my safe place. She put my desk at the front of class, next to hers, and God gave me a real home in a classroom at John Quincy Adams Elementary.

Our young selves hold the keys to our adult pains and anger; therapists call that young self the 'inner child.' I call her 'Baby Girl,' the name I think God uses for me. I was speaking on stage one day when I made that connection. "Oh, my gosh!" I thought. "He was showing up then?" In my darkest days, through Mrs. Bishop, God let me know I was loved, chosen, celebrated, precious, and adored.

Now I can be for others what I needed. I say to clients, "Tune into that baby girl. She knows what thrills you, what calms you, what scares or triggers anger in you." Anger typically is a layer protecting our fear.

As a therapist, I give women what Mrs. Bishop gave me – a safe space to heal, grow, and connect to the full freedom of their identity, their inheritance, as daughters of God. I do it in my Mastermind Groups, when I teach mindful planning, when my husband and I work with couples, when I lead an Instagram Live or go on a Facebook group to talk about your "Hi-5 self." Everything I do leads to the core concept that, "What she does flows out of who she believes she is."

I'm joyfully married now, a mother of eight—every child a miracle since my bout with cancer. Foster care and adoption are wonderfully imperfect. There's not a parenting manual in sight, but an abundance of miracles, mistakes, forgiveness, and a lot of hope. The very same things needed that God used to heal my relationship with my parents.

My husband and I began a nonprofit therapy retreat center on Lake Texoma to bring more healing to more families—to more 'baby girls.'

As a therapist, I go back to that little me who felt like a disappointment and was desperate to be loved. "You are not the problem," I tell her. "You were never the problem. But you damn sure will be the solution."

And I will be.

I'll heal and grow to my last day, taking healing, growth, and God's unconditional love and peace to as many women as I possibly can.

About Stacey

As a Licensed Professional Counselor in both Oklahoma and Texas and a keynote speaker, Stacey Johnson works with women to practice and use their voice, vision, and wildfire faith to create and maintain life change and legacy-driven purpose. She is an author, business mentor, and the lively podcast host of *The Stacey J Show*. Through her virtual mastermind collectives, therapy retreats and intensives for women and couples, Stacey cultivates a life changing, experiential healing process for women, couples, and families. Most recently, in 2022, Stacey founded the GO GET HER conference, a healing experience for women in a vibrant atmosphere of vision and connection.

The core of Stacey's life work stems from one truth: **What she does flows out of who she believes she is.** Using identity as the focus, Stacey works to re-align, re-imagine, and restore the whole self to the fullest and most free expression of worth and power that has always been our true inheritance!

Stacey resides in Dallas, TX with her husband/best friend and power partner, Chris Johnson. They have eight miracle children, six of which were adopted. Together, they own Blume HQ, a creative event space in the heart of Dallas, Texas, and recently founded Magnify Retreat and Conference Center, a nonprofit for healing and growth experiences on a breathtaking 60 acres of waterfront land coming to Lake Texoma to serve individuals, couples, families, leaders, and groups from both Texas and Oklahoma, and beyond!

"I exist to serve my family and equip, empower, and celebrate women in every season. My jam is creating safe spaces for extraordinary healing, growth and connection that restore women to live in the full experience of their true identity and inheritance as Royal daughters!"

Learn more at

- www.staceyjohnson.life